ARAB DAWN

Arab You~~th~~ ... ~~D~~emog~~r~~aph~~ic~~
Divid~~e and What~~ ~~T~~h~~e~~y ~~W~~ill ~~B~~ring

In the West, news about the Middle East is dominated by an endless stream of reports and commentary about civil war, sectarian violence, religious extremism, and economic stagnation. But do they tell the full story? For instance, who knew that university enrolment in the war-torn Palestinian territories exceeds that of Hong Kong, or that more than a third of Lebanese entrepreneurs are women?

Change is on its way in the Middle East, argues Bessma Momani, and its cause is demographic. Today, one in five Arabs is between the ages of fifteen and twenty-four. Young, optimistic, and increasingly cosmopolitan, their generation will shape the region's future. Drawing on interviews, surveys, and other research conducted with young people in fifteen countries across the Arab world, Momani describes the passion for entrepreneurship, reform, and equality among Arab youth. With insightful political analysis based on the latest statistics and first-hand accounts, *Arab Dawn* is an invigorating study of the Arab world and the transformative power of youth.

(UTP Insights)

BESSMA MOMANI is an associate professor in the Department of Political Science at the University of Waterloo and the Balsillie School of International Affairs, a senior fellow at the Centre for International Governance Innovation, and a 2015 fellow at the Pierre Elliott Trudeau Foundation.

UTP Insights

UTP Insights is an innovative collection of brief books offering accessible introductions to the ideas that shape our world. Each volume in the series focuses on a contemporary issue, offering a fresh perspective anchored in scholarship. Spanning a broad range of disciplines in the social sciences and humanities, the books in the UTP Insights series contribute to public discourse and debate and provide a valuable resource for instructors and students.

BOOKS IN THE SERIES

- Bessma Momani, *Arab Dawn: Arab Youth and the Demographic Dividend They Will Bring*
- Stephen M. Saideman, *Adapting in the Dust: Lessons Learned from Canada's War in Afghanistan*
- William Watson, *The Inequality Trap: Fighting Capitalism Instead of Poverty*
- Phil Ryan, *After the New Atheist Debate*
- Paul Evans, *Engaging China: Myth, Aspiration, and Strategy in Canadian Policy from Trudeau to Harper*

ARAB DAWN

Arab Youth and the Demographic Dividend They Will Bring

Bessma Momani

UNIVERSITY OF TORONTO PRESS
Toronto Buffalo London

ISBN 978-1-4426-5065-7 (cloth)
ISBN 978-1-4426-2856-4 (paper)

Publication cataloguing information is available from Library and Archives Canada.

University of Toronto Press acknowledges the financial assistance to its publishing program of the Canada Council for the Arts and the Ontario Arts Council, an agency of the Government of Ontario.

Canada Council
for the Arts

Conseil des Arts
du Canada

ONTARIO ARTS COUNCIL
CONSEIL DES ARTS DE L'ONTARIO

an Ontario government agency
un organisme du gouvernement de l'Ontario

Funded by the
Government
of Canada

Financé par le
gouvernement
du Canada

Contents

Acknowledgments

The sight of millions of young Arabs pouring into public squares to demand positive political, economic, and social change was an inspiring moment in time for me, as for many other people around the world. In the exciting weeks before the overthrow of Hosni Mubarak, young women and men camped out in Cairo's Tahrir Square to devise a progressive constitution, a schedule to pick up garbage in the square, organize sleeping shifts for designated security guards, encircle Muslim and Christian prayers to prevent the intrusion of police forces, and implement critical media messaging to their fellow citizens and the world. They self-organized the square in a remarkable fashion even as the streets of Cairo remained as chaotic, garbage strewn, and unsafe as ever. Looking at Egypt today, did these youth fail or were they merely premature? Only time will tell, but one thing is certain: this generation of Arab youth did something remarkable, and they are not finished, because their expectations of what a good society looks like have yet to materialize.

I owe a great deal of gratitude to the young people who took to the streets, online media, and rooftops to demand change. This book is meant to honour their experiences and voices as best I can. I extend my appreciation to the young people I spoke to in Morocco, Egypt, Jordan, and the United Arab Emirates, and to Syrian and Saudi students studying abroad. In the process of writing this book, especially as I live in the West, I had moments of doubt and sadness about the prospects for change in the region. To remedy this, I went there, talked to young people, and became energized by their amazing stories and experiences. They have high expectations, as they should, and they are working so hard to overcome difficult domestic and regional circumstances. The region is not a lost cause – far from it.

I also had the opportunity to speak to many government officials across the region: royal court advisers, ministers, ambassadors, senators, and civil servants. I thank them for their time and candour, but I have not quoted or cited most of them to protect their identity. To the professors I spoke to in Morocco, Jordan, Egypt, and the UAE, thank you for your time and patience. I realize how privileged I am to practise my craft at a Canadian university, where one truly has freedom of thought.

As a professor at the University of Waterloo and the Balsillie School of International Affairs, I am surrounded by talented people who inspired and encouraged me to write this book. It might be increasingly rare in academic departments, but Waterloo's Department of Political Science is truly a wonderful, nice, and collegial one for which I am most grateful. To walk down the hall and bounce ideas off friends such as Andy Cooper, Eric Helleiner, Kathy Hochstetler, David Welch, and so many of the other talented professors in my department is a blessing. At the Balsillie School, I have similarly had the pleasure of thinking through some of the ideas in this book with friends such as Simon Dalby, Patricia Goff, Jenna Hennebry, and Andrew Thompson.

I am also grateful for comments and feedback from friends and colleagues who read the book, page for page, and gave me much food for thought. Specific thanks to Asim Ali, Andy Cooper, Nathan Funk, Tanzeel Hakak, Dan Herman, Rohinton Medhora, Xenia Menzies, Andrew Thompson, and my editor Daniel Quinlan for their feedback and valuable time. I also very much appreciated and welcomed feedback from anonymous reviewers. Thanks as well for the research support of Cindy Phan, Amanda Sadowski, and Keegan Williams. Thanks to copy editor Barry Norris, whom I had the pleasure of working with again, and to the University of Toronto Press staff and its managing editor, Anne Laughlin.

In the era of social media, I also want to thank my "Twitter cousins," to borrow a term from Amy Hawthorne, who remind me that I am not alone as an analyst and watcher of the Arab world, and that, despite all the challenges, the youth of the Middle East are the hope of the region.

Thank you to my family, extended and near, for their patience. The support of my husband and children is what gave me strength to write something that seemed like an unending project and on a subject that seemed so depressing.

Finally, I want to dedicate this book to Hamza Ali Al-Khateeb, a thirteen-year-old boy from Daraa, Syria, who should have had a bright future ahead of him. For the millions of Syrian children who have paid the price of an oppressive and cruel regime as victims and refugees, I pray that the prognostics of this book come true. After all, Arab youth deserve better than to be seen as enemies of the state; they are a demographic dividend that needs to be nurtured.

ARAB DAWN

Arab Youth and the Demographic
Dividend They Will Bring

chapter one

Introduction

In the West, the Arab region of the Middle East and North Africa is all too often associated with terrorism, religious fanaticism, intolerance, sexism, racism, and a myriad other social and political ills. As a frequent traveller to many of these countries, I get all of the curious questions from border security people in the West. I tell them I am both a professor studying the Arab region and a tourist visiting family and friends there. On many occasions this response is met with bewilderment, and sometimes a hint of disdain. Once, as I transited through London's Heathrow Airport after a trip to the region, the man at the counter declared what most border services people politely refrain from saying: "Madam, you have all of the wrong stamps in your passport." It is my hope that this book will disprove him and others for whom little more than violence and turmoil come to mind when they think of the "Middle East" or the "Arab world."

For those looking for a book that validates their anxieties and misgivings about the Arab region, this is not it. I do not dismiss the real security challenges the region poses, or its vital geostrategic role in international politics. But there is no shortage of books on why and how the Arab region is a security challenge and a hotbed of radical religious views, and it is not my intention, here or anywhere, to add to that list.

For the cover of my first book on the Middle East – a volume about diplomatic relations with the region and having little to do with violence and insecurity – my publisher proposed an image of barbed wire and military men standing in the background, which the marketing representative assured me would offer "a mental shortcut for readers. They'll know this is a book about the Middle East." She might have been right about the perception many people have about the region, but the image is all wrong, and a constant reminder to me of the myopic vision we in the West have of the Arab world.

There is much to be concerned about in the Middle East and North Africa, a region undergoing dramatic change – in many ways the "Arab Spring" was just the beginning of the transformation. Too often, however, the Arab region is written about as a glass half-empty, and one that is draining at that. This book is about the other half of the glass: a young region full of hope, ready for progress, and eager for a bright and prosperous future. Undoubtedly some will criticize this characterization as naive or anecdotal, that I picked only the good stories and the helpful data. But my grandmother taught me a great Arabic proverb that is the core of why this book has value: "Add a hair to another hair, and you eventually get a beard." Sometimes we need to note the region's positive stories, anecdotal events, and initiatives, because something more is taking shape – a story interwoven and held strong by many different strands.

As an academic, I do not expect my findings and stories to reveal any definitive conclusions about the future of the Arab region. I also do not want to sugarcoat the structural challenges that underpin it: real problems are hindering the region's efforts to move forward, and in the conclusion I suggest policies that need to be implemented if it is to realize its potential. I am also not attempting to meet the social scientist's gold standard of a tight methodological study: reading Paul Krugman has taught me that, unless academics put aside their tendency to want to prove a thesis beyond a shadow of a doubt, we can never be relevant and influential public intellectuals. So, here I put aside the academic impulse to support and confirm theory, and showcase the young people I have met in the Arab region who give me such great hope for its future.

To hear their voices, I conducted in-country focus groups in Morocco, Egypt, and Jordan, and with students from Saudi Arabia,

Syria, and Qatar who were in Canada temporarily. I also attended conferences and meetings on the challenges facing youth in the United Arab Emirates (UAE). As well, I interviewed university students from Morocco, Egypt, Jordan, Syria, Lebanon, Saudi Arabia, and the UAE either in the region, via Skype, or at global conferences and meetings. So as not to succumb to a selection bias, I also attempted to speak to youth from rural, poorer, and underfranchised communities, and to those who lacked postsecondary education. Some "interviews" were impromptu meetings with young people in malls, train stations, and lots of taxis and buses. My preferred comfort zone would have been to speak to them in a Starbucks, but I tried to approach young people in all sorts of places and from all walks of life to obtain a well-rounded perspective of their thoughts and aspirations. I was frankly surprised that, despite their differences, youth from across the socio-economic and educational attainment spectrum often shared much of the same outlook. To broaden the reader's perspective of the region and to provide a sense of how Arab youth think and feel about life there, I complement these stories with the results of surveys conducted by academics and policy institutes. Of course, I acknowledge the reality that attitudinal change does not necessarily lead to fundamental political change.

Where possible, I examine and discuss regional differences – clearly, youth in relatively progressive Lebanon and those in religiously conservative Saudi Arabia do not share the same life experience in their views about cosmopolitanism. Still, as an expert on the Arab world with an understanding of the region's subcultural nuances, I was surprised by the similarity of views across the region.

Finally, I had the opportunity to meet with government officials, academics, policy analysts, and international civil servants who work on issues pertaining to the Arab world and, where attribution allows, I quote them directly.

Although this book is not a classic academic study, I hope I have woven the threads into something that gives the reader a better understanding of the Arab region. It is because of these young people that there is reason to see a positive political, economic, and social future for the region. This matters to all of us as global citizens. As a political economist, I see value in the stories and experiences of Arab youth, and I want to tell them and contextualize them within topics of global importance. Indeed, what is happening right now in the Arab region has implications for globalization, economic trade, international diplomacy, business development, demographics, democratization, urbanization, immigration, environmental protection, and cultural production – to name just a few issues.

If, like me, you felt proud of the young people who took to squares and promenades throughout the Arab world in 2011, then feel comfort in knowing that this is generation is the majority of the Arab population, and its members are the region's future leaders and decision-makers. Their thirst for political accountability and an end to corruption, for meritocracy, decent productive work, and social justice, makes me confident about their future. I believe the Arab world eventually will become economically prosperous societies that are also democratic and just. Not long ago, after all, chaos prevailed throughout Europe: in my father's generation, that region was mired in economic disarray, ethnic cleansing, sectarian conflict, and international rivalry. In my early days in graduate school, I was repeatedly told that the Middle East and North Africa were "boring regions to study." Had I not taken the advice of an insightful professor, I would have become a specialist in Latin America, where all of the action was in the 1980s and 1990s, with civil wars, *coups d'état*, economic populism, and desperate experiments in both socialism and capitalism. Now it is the Arab world's turn, and if its youth believe that "the best days are ahead," that is reason enough to keep an open mind about the region.

Who Are They?

It is not easy to define "Arab." Is the term linguistic, cultural, historical, or geographical? Add the complexity of the twenty-two countries that belong to the Arab League, the often interchangeable use of "Middle East" and "North Africa," and the multilingual, multicultural, and multireligious reality of the Arab world, and it becomes still more challenging to arrive at an acceptable definition. Moreover, the term "Arab" is both inclusionary and exclusionary. To me, personally, the Arab region is a fascinating tapestry of different ethnic, cultural, religious, and linguistic communities in which Arabic is the dominant language. Yet, sadly, the emigration of minorities and the imposition of Arabic language and culture by authoritarian regimes is increasing the region's homogeneity. The rise of militant and extremist groups that swear allegiance to a perverse interpretation of Islam – one that does not resonate among the majority of the Arab people – is also blamed for making the social environment for religious minorities less tolerable. Minorities from other ethnic and cultural traditions – Assyrians, Armenians, Chechens, Berbers, Kurds, among many – have not always found the Arab world to be hospitable to "otherness," and it is refreshing to see academic studies that today are rediscovering and chronicling their cultural traditions and stories.

That said, this book needs to have borders, both physical and imaginary. I use the terms "Arab region," "Arab world," "Middle East and North Africa," and "Middle East" interchangeably, although I always mean a recognized set of countries that deem themselves to be predominantly Arab. Of course, this excludes important countries in the Middle East in which Arabs are the minority: Turkey, Iran, and Israel. I also exclude countries that few Arabs would identify as Arab or that speak Arabic, but are nonetheless part of the Arab League: Djibouti, Mauritania, the Comoros, and Somalia. Invariably, therefore, I resort to some degree of generalization in an effort to understand broader trends.

It is not a simple matter to say who is a "youth," either, as the definition varies from country to country and from culture to culture in the region. In theory it is the period between the end of children's dependence on their parents and when, as adults, they gain full employment and become independent. In cultural terms it is that period when society regards an individual as neither a child nor an adult. In some cultures, adulthood is achieved when one moves out of one's parents' home; in others, it is when one gets married. Is a couple that marries at age nineteen still "youth"? Is a twenty-seven-year-old who still lives at home with her parents?

Moreover, the world over, youth increasingly depend on their parents well into adulthood, even as they gain some measure of employment. Clearly, then, "youth" is a concept that depends on the global economy and on shifting social values. For simplicity's sake, I use the common definition of those between the ages of fifteen and twenty-four, unless noted otherwise. Many of the surveys and all of my interviews were of individuals in this age bracket.

By some estimates, the Arab region has the world's youngest population. In 2010 youth were 20 per cent of the Arab world's population; by 2030, despite declining birthrates and smaller families, they will still account for 17 per cent. Who are these youth, and what important role are they playing in Arab society and in the world? Demographically, it is useful to compare sub-Saharan Africa with the Arab region. Many in the business community are optimistic about sub-Saharan Africa because of its young population – indeed, that region's gains in innovation, entrepreneurial spirit, and from the ending of numerous civil wars and conflicts are more reasons to be optimistic. Cover stories from major Western magazines with headlines such as "How Africa Is Becoming the New Asia" nonetheless argue that Africa's success story has been ignored. Prominent economists, including Paul Collier, William Easterly, and Dambisa Moyo, make the bestseller lists by highlighting the myopic thinking of the Western and international aid community towards African economic development. The image of poverty-stricken Africa and the Hollywood awareness campaigns of Bono, Madonna, and Oprah, economists and business people argue, offer only a one-sided picture of the region: Africa is experiencing a boom thanks to the private sector, both foreign and domestic. Yet, even though it is not easy to be optimistic about the Arab world, and harder still to be sanguine about the role of its youth, I contend that the region has better socio-economic indicators and higher educational achievement than sub-Saharan Africa.

Political theorists and pundits often view youth as a problem. In descriptions of the political involvement or activism of youth, one often sees such phrases as "youth bulge" or "youth quake." Clearly, bulges and quakes rarely instil happy thoughts. Too many youth at any one place or time easily conjures up images of gangs, restlessness, and street kids – images that are further reinforced by the media, leading many politicians to be wary of how to deal with them. It might be a generalization to say that youth are rarely viewed as an important segment of society, but too often political leaders fail to view politically active youth as a potential source of votes or as an organizational vehicle for democratic outreach. To a certain extent, the 2008 election of Barack Obama as US president raised interest in youth activism and tools such as social media, but there is still an entrenched, widely held perception that the demands of youth should be contained or curtailed – a view that unfortunately endures in the corridors of power in many countries of the Arab world, and perhaps in the West as well.

This perception has its representatives in the academic community. In political theory, many classic studies try to identify the breaking point – the point at which the presence of too many youth leads to violence or chaos. Samuel Huntington, a prominent political theorist commenting on the developing world – and later in his career a public intellectual who brought the "clash of civilizations" thesis to popular attention – noted that "young people are the protagonists of protest, instability, reform, and revolution."[1] Building on the works of another prominent political historian, Jack Goldstone, viewed as the godfather of writing on revolutions, Huntington predicted that the peak of the youth population in the Muslim world would lead to protest and revolution, and argued that youth bulges could explain both the Iranian Revolution of 1979 and political protests in Algeria in 1992. Pundits such as Fouad Ajami interpret Huntington's views as warning against rising Islamic fundamentalism among Muslim youth. Many theories oppose Huntington's argument and point to a host of other factors to explain these two momentous events and the rise of Islamist politics in general, but it is the underlying assumption that youth undermine political stability to which I object. Perhaps, had Huntington lived to reflect on the Arab Spring, he might have been caught up in the initial euphoria of the crowds in Cairo's Tahrir Square and expanded on one of his underexplored insights: "The rapid expansion of literacy in Arab societies also creates a gap between a literate younger generation and a largely illiterate older generation and thus a 'dissociation between knowledge and power' likely to put a strain on political systems." Translation: an educated, hyperconnected, intelligent Arab youth is coming, which will not tolerate being told by elders that their society is not ready for democracy, accountability, and modernity. This, in my opinion, is the Arab Spring at its very core.

What Do They Want?

Talking to Arab youth about their desires, perspectives, and attitudes was a gratifying experience. Perhaps, as an educator of young adults, I believe that I learn as much from my students as I hope they learn from me. The days when academics lectured and effectively preached from a podium to a mass of students are over. Some attribute this to lower attention spans and the need for constant stimulation among today's students; as one colleague put it, "if you don't become Madonna on tour, you've lost your crowd." But I think today's youth simply learn better when they interact and reflect, rather than memorize and repeat. This is the essence of the development of "critical thinking" skills. Listening to young people is a professional must for me, and I hope I have brought this spirit of "active learning" to the writing of this book.

So, what do young Arabs believe? What do they want? When millions of Egyptians took to the streets during the January 2011 revolution, the phrase they chanted was "bread, freedom, and justice!" In Libya, Syria, and Yemen, Arab youth shouted "down with the regime!" and "we demand respect!" – simple slogans that represented so much more: a fulfilment of the dreams of many and a loss of faith in the ability of their governments to keep up with their rising expectations. In organizing the chapters of this book, I have deconstructed these slogans to capture the way Arab youth see their realities, in stark contrast to previous generations, and the many shortcomings they see in their governments. Arab youth are tackling economic, political, and social failings in creative and innovative ways, and this makes me optimistic about the future of the Arab world.

In Chapter 2 I talk about Arab youth's calls for "bread!" – shorthand for economic dignity and productive work. Arab youth are predominantly educated, and the number of university graduates is growing faster in the Arab world than anywhere else. Many Arab youth are members of what Richard Florida has termed the "creative class": the socio-economic group of workers who effectively create and sell their ideas, knowledge, and innovations in high-value-added professions. Despite common misperceptions, the Arab world ranks relatively high on scales measuring this creative class, which includes more than one in five workers in many Arab countries, including Saudi Arabia, the UAE, Qatar, and Syria. In contrast, in China, another area that looms large in the popularized Western imagination, less than 10 per cent of the workforce is in the creative class, leading some to argue that, while China can copy and produce iPhones, it lacks the human capital to create and innovate. Consider that university enrolment in the war-torn Palestinian territories exceeds that of Hong Kong. When we look across the Arab world, the percentage of youth enrolled in university is remarkable: Libya and Lebanon, for instance, have youth enrolment rates close to Canada's.[2]

Still, although there is no shortage of young, educated Arabs, many remain unemployed or underemployed after graduation, and face many challenges when seeking opportunities to take advantage of their education. These challenges include a corrupt political and social system rife with nepotism and family networks that stunt the ability of talented youth to compete on the basis of meritocracy. The barriers are even higher for Arab women: even though female university graduates outnumber male graduates in the Arab world, female unemployment is sometimes double that of men.[3]

Lacking more conventional options, young Arabs are turning to entrepreneurship as never before. It is a way for many young Arab women, in particular, to challenge sexism in the workplace. Although globally only 10 per cent of entrepreneurs are women, in Lebanon women account for more than a third of the country's entrepreneurs.[4] Many of the young women and men I spoke to are aspiring entrepreneurs who look up to new national champions in the private sector and have much to say about how to propel and modernize domestic and regional economies. Thus, in Chapter 2, I highlight how their entrepreneurial spirit and innovative ideas are challenging the nepotistic old guard and explain why demographics is propelling them to success.

In Chapter 3 I talk about "freedom," and examine how youth think about government and politics – specifically, how they have taken to online forums to challenge the political status quo. Unlike previous generations, who were willing to accept the rule of "strongmen," today's Arab youth are searching for leaders who can get things done. For far too long, the notion that Arabs want to be ruled by strongmen prevailed in policy circles, particularly in Washington. I have never found this argument helpful in explaining the politics of the region, not the least because it typically descends into cultural arguments about how the Arab people respect the abuser, or that they simply view "might as right." It is a popular view that is too reminiscent of cultural psychologist Raphael Patai's 1973 book, *The Arab Mind*, which provided lessons on how to dominate Arabs, and implied that such lessons were legitimated by the behaviour of Arabs themselves. When Seymour Hersh wrote his exposé in the *New Yorker* about the abuse of Iraqi prisoners in the Abu Ghraib prison, he noted that Patai's book was the inspiration behind the Bush neoconservatives' *modus operandi* for containing the Arab people. The book, like Abu Ghraib, is a reminder of the various ways in which Arabs have been dehumanized by outside analysts.

The Arab Spring debunked this "strongmen" view once and for all. The uprisings were devoid of charismatic leaders, and none has captured the imagination of the various revolutions thus far. To be sure, the international community called for the revolutionary groups to find leaders so that external powers would have interlocutors. Frankly, Arab youth are not searching for new larger-than-life leaders. They are not looking for someone to take to the podium and rhyme off speeches that try to restore confidence with rhetoric and empty promises. Arabs – youth, in particular – do not want to pay deference to strongmen, real or perceived. They are fed up with omnipotent leaders. So, when President Mohamed

Morsi spoke to the Egyptian nation and President Bashar al-Assad stood in front of the Damascus Opera House to give his statesmen a lesson in geopolitics, they were completely out of sync with the dynamic of these youth-led revolutions.

The Arab uprisings showed that the fiery speeches of the past that referred to the old binary of "us versus them" and pointed to an ominous enemy no longer satisfy Arab youth, who have access to information and analysis from around the world. Arab youth want accountable government that delivers prosperity, not one that justifies its existence on the basis of an outside enemy. Long-winded speeches and convoluted ideological arguments do not satisfy an educated, well-travelled, and increasingly cosmopolitan people. Arabs want leaders who will combat corruption and nepotism. They want reform in every sense of the word.

In Chapter 4 I talk about "identity" and how Arab youth view themselves and their place in society. Arab governments, clerics, elders, and the state-controlled media have long projected an image of a respectful, pious society that citizens should emulate. Indeed, for many Arab youth, the search for dignity and justice has heightened their Islamic faith. Unlike clerics in the pulpit, however, Arab youth do not view their identity in oppositional terms of believers and non-believers. Rather, their religious practice takes shape in a fusion: Arab youth want to be both Western and persons of faith. They are tired of governments that view their religiosity as a political threat, and use the rise of political Islam as an excuse for political autocracy and repression. Yet, political Islam is not to be confused with the "radicalization of Muslims in the name of Islam," as in the barbarity and terror of the so-called Islamic State. Political Islam can be movements and parties that base their ideology on the teachings of Islam, but explicitly want to work within a democratic political system. Undoubtedly many within and outside the region have their suspicions about political Islamic groups and parties such as the region-wide Muslim Brotherhood. Critics of political Islam believe that these parties and movements also want to install a theocratic state in the long term, but that is a bigger debate beyond the scope of this book. For our purposes, political Islam is deemed movements and parties that renounce violence, that want to seek political power and voice through the ballot box, and that agree to participate in future elections once in power. In ideal terms, the future of political Islamic movements will resemble the Christian democratic parties of Europe. They are not there yet, but they also have not been tested or tried in the Arab world. Political Islam is a far cry from the radicalization of groups such as al-Qaeda and ISIS, which capture and dominate headlines in current media accounts of conflict in the Middle East. For many Arab youth, turning to spirituality can be an important way to positive self-reflection in a system corrupted by nepotism, indignity, and economic despair.

The trend towards religiosity in the Arab region need not be equated with intolerance and oppression. The Arab world is rapidly urbanizing, and with this comes a more cosmopolitan identity – that is, where cultural, ethnic, and tribal identities are melding, giving way to diversity and plurality. Too often politicians have used tribal, regional, religious, and ethnic identities to rile up narrow bases of support. Today's young, educated, and modern Arabs increasingly reject these social cleavages. New social movements – from women's Quran-reading clubs to Harley-Davidson riding clubs – are springing up across the region, displacing old and outdated forms of social division. At the same time, Arabs reject the notion that, to be cosmopolitan and modern, they must abandon their religious faith. In many ways, this is the reason for the Arab uprisings – the consequence of the increased education, urbanization, and empowerment of the Arab people. It is hard to tell a generation of young people that because someone else commands the megaphone and has a stick to back it, they ought to acquiesce. The Arab Spring, therefore, should put an end to another prevalent thesis, that of "Arab exceptionalism," whereby Arabs always run counter to modernizing global trends and fail to progress, and that they are merely waiting for new strongmen to replace the old. There has indeed been a resurgence of identities of Islam, the dominant religion throughout the region. But along with the rise of political Islam has been a spiritual revival that attracts Arab youth and women. It is not the draconian "Islamism" of radical and militant groups that takes centre stage in Western media.

As Arab youth rediscover faith in modern ways, they are developing new cosmopolitan identities. Today's Arab youth are likely to have been raised in a city – indeed, the Arab region is one of the most urbanized in the world, and the pace is increasing. Between 1970 and 2010 the urban Arab world grew by 400 per cent, and is expected to increase by another 200 per cent over the next forty years. In 2010, of 357 million people in the Arab world, 56 per cent lived in cities; by 2050, it is projected, of 646 million people in the Arab world, 68 per cent will live in cities.[5] When Arabs leave the countryside, many of the primordial identities of clan, sect, and tribe become less important to them.

In the 1950s many Arabs still intermarried within their own tribe, preferred as a way to keep wealth, land, and kinship in the family. Today, more and more Arab youth are marrying across cultural, ethnic, and tribal lines.[6] Inevitably, this will shape stronger cosmopolitan identities. Moreover, as traditional marriages decline, Arab youth are now predominantly marrying someone they love. One of the most divided Arab societies is Lebanon, where sectarianism is officially embedded in its constitution and in almost every walk of life. Many Lebanese lament that it takes three people to do one person's job: a Christian, a Sunni Muslim, and a Shiite Muslim. Yet, despite these deep fractures, there is strong opposition to such sectarianism on the part of young Lebanese activists, which led, in 2012, to a national debate when young couples began to demand civil marriages that did not register their religious sects. The Lebanese newspaper *Daily Star* reported that nearly eight hundred couples took a one-hour flight to Cyprus to have a civil marriage. The push and final acceptance of a civil marriage law was a coup for young Lebanese who saw the ills of social divisions embedded in the social and political system.

Arab youth's innovation in political mobilization and economic activity is also apparent in their artistic works. The Arab region has seen a surge in the arts, encompassing film, visual art, poetry, and music. Arab youth have found new voices and new, more receptive audiences for their art.[7] The online world has become their sanctuary for progressive and liberal ideals about the society they seek to build. Rejecting binaries, they meld modern, Islamic, and liberal ideas in innovative ways. I hope to showcase their stories and their determination to fight the economic, political, and social divisions of their world.

Why Is This Relevant?

With so much change happening in the region, it is easy to overlook the big picture. If you are in industry, you cannot afford to ignore one of the fastest-growing consumer markets in the world. If you are an engineer, urban planner, designer, marketer, or advertiser, your clients are more likely to be in the growing population of the Arab world than in the aging population of Europe. A young Arab world that challenges economic, political, and social norms matters.

There is an ongoing fascination with predicting shifts in the centres of global power, as evidenced in the works of public intellectuals and popular academics such as Fareed Zakaria, Thomas Freidman, Niall Ferguson, and Paul Kennedy. Today, the future trajectory of economic growth, political power, and arguably even social norms is being shaped by the "decline of the West and rise of the rest." With globalization and declining costs of the dissemination of goods, services, and knowledge, the West can no longer monopolize innovation, capital, and resources. The engine of growth in the global economy has already shifted to "the rest."

The oft-cited example of the iPhone illustrates how production has become globalized in a supply chain that links applications designed around the globe with finance in New York or London, technical know-how in Silicon Valley, assembly lines in Zhengzhou, and over four hundred Apple retail stores worldwide, the largest of which is in Amsterdam. The multinational corporation of the 1980s, which had operations in more than one country, is likely now a transnational corporation without a centralized headquarters and with a workforce that is globally dispersed. It is not just economic production that is globalized, but also knowledge, innovation, and consumption. In 2001, Jim O'Neill, former chairman of Goldman Sachs, famously localized this shift in global economic power to the BRICs: Brazil, Russia, India, and China. A decade later, O'Neill updated this to the MIST: Mexico, Indonesia, South Africa, and Turkey. Today there is no shortage of watch lists, from the CIVETS (Colombia, Indonesia, Vietnam, Egypt, Turkey, and South Africa) to the G20. Although these lists are somewhat faddish, it is important to note that economic growth will be diffused, and with that, so will be political, normative, and cultural power.

Today's generation of educated and interconnected Arab youth cannot be ignored if one is to understand this diffusion of power in the new global landscape, which is not just an economic story, but a demographic story as well. Put simply, the West is aging. An aging population cannot be the source of an efficient labour pool, a creative culture, or a consuming population. It is youth who will innovate, produce, consume, and shape global norms and ideas.

Diffusion of economic power is easy to see and measure, but diffusion of ideas and cultural norms is harder to grasp. Clearly, more products are made in the emerging market economies than ever before, as we see in our everyday lives. I recall my daughter as a young child asking if all of her toys came from the "Made in China" store. It is hard to escape the reality that the global assembly line has moved offshore, but how has political power diffused? In his insightful book, *The End of Power*, Moses Naim discusses how the diffusion of political power looks and feels. In essence the shift is not just from "the West to the rest," because of the economic realities of globalization, but also "from presidential palace to public squares," because of social, normative, and political change in how we communicate and perceive authority. Naim asserts that what we are witnessing is the *decay* of power. Power will be harder to get and harder to hold on to. People everywhere are more demanding, and governments need to be more responsive to their publics than ever before if they are to survive.

In introductory political science, we teach students the basic definition of power: "the ability to get someone to do something he or she would not otherwise do." Decaying power, as Naim conceives it, implies it is more difficult for leaders – be they in political capitals, business boardrooms, or family homes – to get someone to do something he or she would not do. This is partly a function of a generational change in attitudes about power and authority. It is more difficult for me, for instance, to order my children to do something without explaining why I want them to do it. Just as my students do not want to be lectured to, my authority as professor, much like my authority as a mother, has changed. I must convince them that my authority is legitimate through reasoning, not through power or might.

The rise of the rest includes the youth of the Arab world. How will they relate to other societies, especially the West? From local views to potential global impact, in the last chapter I look at the international relevance of the demographic dividend of a young Arab world that is increasingly interconnected with the West and the rest, and how those interconnections will affect the course of global economic, geopolitical, and cultural relations.

The cultural influences of the West in the Arab region and of the Arab and Muslim identities in Western multicultural societies cannot be ignored. The Arab world is increasingly a source of immigrants, workers, and talent in Western countries, which presents both an opportunity, in terms of economic and cultural ties, and a challenge to old concepts or images of the "other." With hundreds of thousands of Arab students having already returned from the West with postsecondary degrees, a host of public Arab diplomats are carrying new values and ideas that will shape the future of their countries. Arab youth will take advantage of a society that is experiencing circularity, one in which it can no longer be assumed that the flow of people, money, and ideas is simply one way: from the rest to the West. How will this transnational movement of students, workers, and migrants affect the Arab region?

Finally, I tackle two questions. First, what about the surge of violence and sectarianism in the Arab world? Second, what policy proposals would help Arab youth further their successes? Arab and Western policymakers need to overcome certain policy challenges to harness the economic, social, and political development that is the promise of the Arab world's demographic dividend. A common policy challenge across the Arab region will be to promote productive and inclusive economic growth that employs its talented youth. Some Arab countries will have greater success than others in realizing the fruit of the demographic dividend. The oil-rich Gulf states will be the principal regional investors; more populous countries such as Egypt and Morocco are likely to expand their manufacturing, and smaller countries such as Lebanon, Jordan, the Palestinian territories, and Tunisia could be the creative core. The Arab Spring has made youth's success a political imperative as well. Arab political leaders know they need to provide jobs or share the fate of the ousted autocrats.

As this book will show, Arab youth are an increasingly empowered public, and global trends do not favour a long-term return to authoritarian rule. Empowered Arab youth can also be a political challenge if they are not given a genuine opportunity to participate in building their societies. It cannot be ignored that too many young people are affected by violence emanating from the region, but it is imperative that Arab leaders not add fuel to the fire by using sectarian tropes and narratives. Media headlines about fighting terrorism in the region are real, but how the vast majority of Arab youth live and think about their homelands and the world is rarely captured in these vignettes. I hope this book fills that void.

chapter two

Bread

When the Arab Spring broke out in 2010, a perfect storm of economic pressures affecting Arab youth was already brewing. With an international financial crisis in full swing, the Arab world faced drastic rises in food and energy prices, reduced access to international credit, and government-slashed public support and services. Yet, the way Arab youth thought about work, economic dignity, and their relationship with the state changed in the previous two decades, a period in which young people witnessed the weakening of public services and the rise of private enterprise.

It is futile to try to find a definitive reason for the widespread adoption of economic liberalization that occurred in the Middle East throughout the 1990s and 2000s. Rather, economic liberalization is better explained as an outcome of the spread of neoliberal ideas over the period. Throughout the 1990s, many Arab countries removed government subsidies, opened foreign investment opportunities, and shrank the public sector. At times these policies were driven by an intense need for loans from global financial institutions such as the International Monetary Fund and World Bank, which often carried with them tough conditions. Arab governments were also encouraged by Western donor agencies that used their aid dollars to promote free market economies throughout the region.

The Arab elite felt this move towards greater market liberalization as well. Indeed, influenced by the talk in the halls of power – including, for example, in the exclusive clubs of the World Economic

Forum – of the glories of the free market, many Arab leaders willingly and enthusiastically tried to adopt liberal economic policies. Some saw private enterprise as a way to help benefit their families or inner circles. Arab officials and decision-makers, many trained in economics and business in Western universities, also touted the virtues of the free market. The pursuit of these neoliberal policies also changed how today's Arab youth believe government should relate to citizens and how economic prosperity should be achieved. With economic liberalization, Arab youth have begun to challenge their societies' autocratic style of governance.

The 1990s and 2000s: Decades of Economic Liberalization

At the national level, economic liberalization involved a relaxation of barriers that once prevented global trade, foreign investment, and private enterprise. Legal reforms allowed, then encouraged, foreign companies to export goods to the Arab world and to set up local offices and branches. Many of these reforms were mandated by Arab countries' membership in the World Trade Organization or were developed through bilateral investment and free trade agreements with larger Western countries. The relaxation of investment barriers and corresponding legal reforms also allowed many businesses in Arab countries to compete with national or state-owned companies, thus opening up an economic space that had been sealed off to small business owners and entrepreneurs.

In line with the opening of their borders to new goods, money, and services, Arab governments also began to reduce subsidies for food and rent and easing other price controls, dramatically cut back government services and reduce the size of the public sector by hiring fewer people. As they ushered in economic liberalization, they decreased wages relative to rises in inflation, increased university tuition fees, privatized or liberalized state-owned manufacturing, and privatized a host of government services ranging from waste management to airports and telecoms. Throughout much of the Arab region in the 1990s and 2000s, goods and services that the state once provided for free or at subsidized rates declined rapidly. The overall effect was to increase the price of almost everything. True, the level of service delivery improved, and there was better competition in the private sector, but after two decades of economic liberalization, life in the Arab world had changed enormously. Urban centres, in particular, became increasingly more expensive as food subsidies, rent controls, and other state-provided perks declined. The Arab city became a modern city in the Western sense, but the increasing cost of living there made it difficult to enjoy the city's new amenities. With the transformation, Arab youth today are more exposed to global services and brands than their elders ever were. Perhaps it is a cliché, but many Arab youth grow up eating at McDonalds, shopping at Carrefour, and watching MTV. When I asked young people throughout the Arab region what activities they enjoyed, they often described those of consumption: shopping malls, coffee shops, fast food restaurants, and cinemas that all provided the pleasures of modern life.

In the early 1990s most Arab cities were still relatively untouched by the private sector and consumerism. In the more industrialized countries – such as Egypt, Syria, Algeria, and Iraq – goods were often produced locally by state-owned enterprises. In Damascus, Beirut, and Amman, I saw many people shopping at government outlet stores. Inside, there were no flashy signs – in fact, barely any advertising at all – and the model seemed to be that of the recently departed Soviet Union. Still, such shops had catered for decades to the working middle class, teachers, bureaucrats, and those in the military. For many city dwellers, wages were not high, but most basic goods and services were affordable and their quality fair, leaving many satisfied with their economic lot in life. Today, these shops have almost disappeared. In Arab shops, many of the goods manufactured in the Arab region now must compete with global brands and more cheaply manufactured products from East Asia. For much of the Arab middle class, paying retail market prices for basic goods and services now means incurring a larger burden on the family purse.

It is worth noting the dramatic cuts in public expenditures across the Arab world. To give an example, public spending accounted for 23.6 per cent of the region's gross domestic product (GDP) in the 1980s, 22.1 per cent of GDP in the 1990s, and 17.2 per cent in the 2000s – the sharpest drop in spending on public services among all the developing countries over that period, according to the World Bank.[1] With the decline in public funding has come the deterioration of many services once provided by Arab governments. Perhaps the most notable change is in education, where there is now a demand for parallel private education from primary to university, and in health care, where private facilities increasingly cater to the middle class, who bypass the ailing public system at great cost to their personal savings. In impoverished areas, whose residents cannot afford private alternatives to disappearing government services, other civil society actors have attempted to fill the gap. In Egypt the Muslim Brotherhood ran health care clinics, daycare centres, tutoring services, and other parallel organizations affected by government cutbacks or neglect.[2]

In many other ways, as well, the changes brought on by economic liberalization drastically reoriented the typical Arab city. Before, private retailing in the Middle East was, in the Western sense, highly underdeveloped, with most goods sold in small shops dotted along the older parts of the downtown core. It was quite an experience to venture into an area where similar goods were grouped together in the same street or alleyway; there, one would find a spice section, a clothing alleyway, and an electronics corridor. Locals would frustrate the traveller with such directions as "turn right at the footwear street and then left at the lingerie boulevard," when streets with such names did not actually exist. Formally, streets were often named after a national hero or an individual from the inner circle, but to the people they were known for their function and purpose: what was sold and traded on them.

In late 2010, while working for the Amman Institute, a think tank focused on urban development issues, colleagues and I conducted a number of focus groups of downtown Amman's business owners, who lamented that locals increasingly preferred to drive to large shopping malls, where they could park with ease and shop in air-conditioned comfort. Tourists still flock to the downtown core, but local shoppers, particularly the working middle class and youth, are less interested in the old experience. When we asked groups of young children from middle-class backgrounds to draw "Amman downtown," they tended to draw pictures of traffic jams, car accidents, and kids stuck in cars. For them, the beauty and charm of shopping in the quintessential Arab bazaar had lost its relevance.

The spread of shopping malls in the Middle East has had an enormous impact on local economies and, consequently, on Arab youth. The 2000s saw a spike in the number and size of shopping malls being built throughout the Arab world. Many were financed and developed by Gulf developers, their coffers overflowing after a near-decade-long oil boom. As foreign investment laws began to be relaxed throughout the Arab region, these investors found their own neighbourhood fertile ground for real estate and retail development. Many leaders and the urban elite encouraged this bonanza of malls, high-end office towers, resort villages, and amusement parks. Enchanted by the "Dubai model" of economic development – which emphasizes the glamorous side of urban development centred on consumption and a motto of "build it and they will come" – this burgeoning construction literally changed the skyline of most Arab cities in the 2000s. Throughout the region rose mega-malls such as City Stars and Festival City in Cairo; Mecca Mall, City Mall, and Taj Mall in Amman; and Dubai Mall in the United Arab Emirates (UAE). Gulf investors also poured money into developing Western-like "new downtowns," including Solidère in Beirut, Abdalli in Amman, Jabal Omar in Mecca, and Festival City in Cairo. These new spaces have all of the trappings of Western culture, food, and lifestyle, and although they cater to middle- and upper-class families, they particularly attract youth. Young Arabs stop at Starbucks for a latté, walk the boulevards and malls to shop or browse at the Gap, IKEA, or Gucci, then go bowling or go-carting, or watch the latest blockbuster Hollywood film.

I found malls one of the best places to find Arab youth and start an informal focus group, and I discovered that they often shared a similar attitude towards these spaces. At a mall in Rabat, Morocco, I met with a group of three friends and asked them to share their feelings about this environment. Faten, a bright, articulate, and fluent English-speaking seventeen-year-old from an upper-class socio-economic background, said: "I feel at home in these spaces. We, the youth, have adopted an American style of life in our food, culture, we are open to new things, and when I'm here, I feel like this is my kind of world and meet up with people who share my values." Dana, a twenty-one-year-old student at Jordan's Yarmouk University, said: "My friends and I go to malls because we can spend hours walking in a clean space, with relative security, stop at a café and have an espresso, go into stores and look at the beautiful new fashion trends, having a good time without spending a lot of money." Although Dana and her friends are often welcomed into malls, her brother Ashraf, a twenty-year-old student at Jordanian German University, lamented: "I also like to go to malls, but on weekends I can't enter with my friends. Security guards say we are just hooligans who want to chase girls. I'm not like that, but we boys are always treated badly and perceived to be uncivilized."

The relationship between youth and these new urban developments is, however, mixed. In a region with a notable absence of free public spaces, long periods of hot weather, and diminishing public investment in sports and extracurricular activities, it is no surprise that many youth enjoy gathering and meeting up at the mall to enjoy, in a limited way, some aspects of the Western style of life. Many Arab youth, particularly those from the growing ranks of the unemployed, spend a great deal of time in these new urban spaces, where, for a small but not insignificant amount of money, they can be served in cafés and restaurants. Mainly referring to youth, Jillian Schwedler calls these individuals "aspiring cosmopolitans" whose interaction with symbols of Western culture can have an empowering effect on their sense of self. As Schwedler notes, in these new spaces Arab youth are increasingly able to become comfortable in elite-dominated places and at least play the part of engaging in the benefits of economic liberalization.[3] The flipside of this sense of empowerment is Arab youth's growing awareness of socio-economic inequality. Before malls existed, working-class youth had little knowledge of or insight into how the wealthy spent their money. Throughout the Middle East, exclusive country clubs have been the norm since the time of colonial rule, but few members of the lower class were able to view the mores of the mainly urban elite. Today, rapid urban development has exposed to the public how the Arab elite live, spend, and enjoy their leisure time.

After two decades of economic liberalization, Arab society has changed profoundly. Government officials now tell the people: "Pull yourselves up by your bootstraps and start fending for yourselves." I recall hearing Egyptian President Hosni Mubarak, in the mid-1990s, give a fiery speech to a crowd in a relatively poor part of the country. He literally yelled that Egypt could not afford to subsidize and feed families that chose to have ten children – overpopulation, he claimed, would bankrupt the Egyptian state. Of course, Mubarak failed to note that government spending on the military and security sectors was simultaneously on the rise, or to mention the high rate of corruption and cronyism that was draining the public purse. In later years the message from Arab leaders was similar: "The public purse cannot afford to be used for general societal welfare. You are on your own."

Prior to the two decades of economic liberalization, government expenditures in Arab countries as a percentage of GDP were, on average, higher than in many developed industrialized countries. Moreover, much of this spending was not financed by serious or widespread tax collection. This "autocratic bargain" represented a unique social contract between Arab rulers and their people. Unlike the American Revolution's mantra of "no taxation without representation," the Arab region's social contract was "no representation and no taxation." The message was clear: Arab people should not expect democracy or political liberalization because their governments were taking care of them by dolling out generous social welfare programs and public services, keeping income taxes to a minimum, and leaving the taxation base largely untapped. Today, few Arab youth have memories of generous public services such as subsidized goods and services and the societal expectations they entailed. Consequently, they see no need to hold up their end of the autocratic bargain. How they think about

productive work and economic dignity in an era of economic liberalization is revealing about how they see their place in the changing Arab world.

In Search of Economic Dignity

The self-immolation of twenty-six-year-old Tunisian Mohamed
Bouazizi is often said to have been the spark that set off the Arab
Spring. Less widely understood are the reasons so many of his com-
patriots were moved by his act. Bouazizi was a college-educated
young man without formal employment. He was indebted to cred-
itors for helping to put his sister through university and supporting his mother, and he tried to earn a living selling fruit and
vegetables on a cart in a small town. When a policewoman ha-
rassed him for a bribe in lieu of a vendor's permit, Bouazizi, unable to pay, faced the further indignity of not being able to work at
his meagre $10-a-day job. After the policewoman confiscated his
weigh scales, Bouazizi went to the office of his local governor to
lodge a formal complaint and seek their return. After the local authorities brushed him off, the young man doused himself with fuel
in front of the governor's office and set himself ablaze after yelling,
"How do you expect me to make a living?"[4]

What resonated about Bouazizi's story in the Arab world, especially among its youth, was that he had been trying to do all the
right things: get an education, be entrepreneurial, work within the
system to get ahead in life. Arab youth are increasingly better educated than were previous generations. The opening line of a 2009
Brandeis University report on higher education in the Arab region
could not have been more on the mark: "The Arab world is experiencing a silent yet multidimensional revolution that needs to
be closely assessed: a surge in higher education."[5] The figures are
striking: since the early 2000s the number of universities in the
Arab region has doubled from 178 to 398; if one adds community
colleges and institutes, the number rises to 1,139.[6] This means a
doubling in the number of university graduates, a rate far exceed-
ing that of population growth.

Contributing to the growth of postsecondary education is the rise of private universities, which are now able to set up and compete in the Arab region thanks to economic liberalization – in Bahrain, Lebanon, the Palestinian territories, Qatar, and the UAE, private universities now account for 80 per cent of the total.[7] Foreign universities are also increasingly present in the region. Particularly in the Gulf, American universities such as Georgetown, Cornell, New York University, and many others have built campuses to take advantage of the increased desire and demand of Arab youth for higher education. A number of Gulf countries are also investing enormously in building education cities or hubs. The Qatari government, for example, has poured billions of dollars – nearly 20 per cent of its budget – into the country's education system;[8] the hub is Education City, which houses foreign universities and new policy centres. In the UAE's Dubai International Academic City, branches of nearly three dozen foreign universities take advantage of tax incentives to build campuses to educate tens of thousands. At a cost of $4 billion over the coming decade, Saudi Arabia is building the King Abdullah Education City, a site intended to host a number of primary schools and university campuses to serve 18,000 students and 7,500 faculty recruited from around the world. The increase in universities across the region is remarkable. Yet the rise in the proportion of educated Arab youth is not simply an issue of supply, but an indication of a strengthened ethos that respects educational attainment.

Granted, this culture of respect for higher education is not new to the region's larger cities or to the Arab upper class – universities in Fez, Cairo, Damascus, and Baghdad have been centres of excellence and intellectual thought for more than a hundred years. What is new is the attitude towards higher education in rural areas, where the ethos has flourished with astounding results, and where the pride and joy of many is not material possessions, but the education of their children. In recent visits to rural Jordan, I met elderly women, many illiterate, who proudly boasted that all of their granddaughters had attended university. When I had spoken to many of these same women twenty years ago, they had prided themselves on how much land their families possessed and how all of their daughters had "married well."

One of the more interesting phenomena in the Arab world is the increase in female education. Dana, the twenty-one-year-old lower-middle-class student at Yarmouk University, said: "I find families today worry more about educating their daughters more than their sons, because uneducated men can often find jobs in manual labour, but women who don't get a degree will likely stay home and depend on their parents for financial support." As in many developed economies, in the Arab region more women than men attain a university-level education. In the mid-2000s, meeting students at Al-Ain University – an all-female campus in the UAE – who were studying business management for young entrepreneurs, I listened with fascination as they asked questions and eagerly took notes. Impressively, in the UAE, women outperform men in both high school and university, and account for 70 per cent of all university students.[9] Like the rural women I interviewed in Jordan, Emirati parents, especially mothers, push their daughters to excel at university. Societal and family expectation that a university degree will secure a woman's future and diminish dependency on a husband or male relative is also pushing women to pursue higher education.[10] In my brief time visiting Al-Ain University, I saw a deep desire to learn and succeed, a trait much less pronounced among many of the students I myself have taught for over a decade. To my surprise, in this conservative Gulf state, where the prospects of female employment after graduation are low, were the most enthusiastic learners I'd ever encountered. Remarkably, 77 per cent of Emirati women are university educated, well above rates of achievement in Canada, the United States, and most other industrialized countries.

Despite the increase in the numbers who are university educated, however, in the UAE and elsewhere in the Arab world the employment opportunities for women are bleak. Arab women have the lowest labour force participation rate in the world,[11] and in the Gulf it is even lower than in the rest of the Arab region. In Saudi Arabia, for example, the number of women currently in university outnumbers that of males.[12] Yet, although 60 per cent of university graduates in Saudi Arabia are women, only 15 per cent of women are employed in the Kingdom.[13] When I asked some young Emirati women about their studies and future goals, it became clear to me why they wanted to work so hard and learn and absorb so much, despite their low prospects of employment: they were savouring a moment in time, perhaps one of the few and final in their adult lives, when they could experience true meritocracy, when they could be valued for their skills and intellect, rather than for their family relations. Women across the region share the sentiments of these Emiratis. They crave recognition of their intelligence and talent, yet face a formal employment system that does not offer such satisfaction. Why, then, pursue an education? On this point, Dana stated: "an Arab woman has to get a university degree today. A degree says to the world that you know how to talk, you hold your head up high, you know how to raise your children, and you are confident; without a degree, a woman is lost and will be fooled by men who say they love them because they saw her crossing the street. Those days are gone. We Arab women are more confident and know who we are and what we want." University education thus has status value that is now universal across the region, especially among young women – not as a means to find formal employment but as an end in itself.

As many reports sponsored by international development agencies note, however, the Arab world faces a significant challenge in the mismatch between the increased supply of skills through education and the needs of employers. As well, the quality of higher education in the region is not high: few Arab universities rank highly as global champions or against those in comparator countries of the developing world.[14] The reports also charge that Arab education emphasizes rote memorization and does not foster critical thinking skills, and that there are too many university graduates at the expense of vocational training. In my own assessment of Arab academics' publications and incentives to excel, it was clear that few universities in the region have internalized the "publish or perish" mantra that keeps many of my colleagues on a treadmill of work and research.[15]

On the surface, many real and deep reforms are needed to improve Arab university systems, but this misses the point: educated Arab youth believe they are prepared for, and deserving of, productive employment. In a 2005 poll of young Arabs, the vast majority of respondents believed they were unemployed because "jobs don't exist." This was followed by "nepotism and corruption" and, near the bottom of the list, "education doesn't prepare" as reasons for low youth employment rates.[16] It is the perception of the unemployed that they are prepared to work that is key here, and that helps to explain why Arab youth called for revolution in the Arab Spring.

In one sense, it is puzzling that Arab youth led the charge. On the whole, Arab economies were not doing too badly, particularly compared with those of other developing regions.[17] Ironically, however, the revolts began in countries with economies that were growing at a reasonable clip: Tunisia, at 3 per cent and 4 per cent GDP growth in 2009 and 2010, respectively; Egypt, at 4.7 per cent and 5 per cent; Libya, at 1.8 per cent and 5.2 per cent; Yemen, at 3.9 per cent and 7.8 per cent; and Syria, at 4 per cent and 5 per cent.[18] Some Gulf states had growth rates in the double digits and, thanks to oil prices that hovered above $100 per barrel for nearly a decade, they amassed capital wealth to the tune of a trillion dollars.[19] The Arab region's growth rates would have been the envy of any developed economy, particularly on the heels of the international financial crisis of 2008. Most Arab governments were not highly leveraged or connected to international financial creditors and banks. When short-term drops in oil prices threw off their budget planning, they were not affected for long.

As well, many Arab countries were experiencing modest growth in income per capita, and inequality gaps were narrowing throughout the region:[20] according to some measures, Arab countries were more egalitarian than those in Latin America and sub-Saharan Africa, and comparable to those in East Asia.[21] That said, comparisons of inequality based on household consumption patterns are criticized because wealthy individuals might underreport their income and spending habits – a survey of Egyptians using a different measure revealed, in contrast, a growing gap between rich and poor in that country.[22] Another measure, income per capita, also showed improvement throughout the region, although not nearly as quickly as in Asia or Latin America, particularly among the middle class.[23] Finally, employment growth rates in the Arab region, at 3.3 per cent per year from 1998 to 2008, were the highest in the world.[24]

In sum, the economic data tell a story of improvement throughout the Arab world over two decades of economic liberalization. But herein lies the dilemma for a solely economic analysis of the Arab Spring: it cannot help us understand why Arab youth long for a better life and why they led the calls for revolution. Simply put, Arab youth supported the Arab Spring because they believed they *deserved better*.

To put this in theoretical terms, Ted Gur's 1970 book, *Why Men Rebel*, is insightful. Gurr developed a useful argument to explain rebelliousness, encapsulated in a term he called "relative deprivation," where there is a "tension that develops from a discrepancy between the 'ought' and the 'is' of collective value satisfaction."[25] Akin to Gurr's argument, the Arab Spring was a moment when Arab youth said to themselves, "I've done all of the right things, I deserve better than my economic, political, and social lot, and I know and see what I deserve to have." Again, the concept of "relative deprivation" suggests that it is not absolute poverty or lack of economic growth or even income inequality that leads people to rebel but the prize of socio-economic prosperity, which they see before them and say, *I deserve that.* "Relative deprivation" explains many of the attitudes and values of the Arab youth I met.

Nevertheless, economic grievances – particularly the challenge of finding meaningful employment based on merit – clearly are a large part of the puzzle in understanding Arab youth's motivations for supporting the Arab Spring. Youth unemployment in the Arab region is the highest in the world,[26] and their labour force participation rate, at 35 per cent compared with 52 per cent in the rest of the world, is the lowest. Even more staggering is the rate of "underemployment," where the educated take jobs below their qualifications in order to earn money – the cliché of the Cairo taxi driver with a medical degree is sadly true. Cross-national surveys have led many analysts to believe that official unemployment rates, in fact, are underreported, and that they are actually closer to 35 to 40 per cent.[27] Corruption and nepotism also thwart productive people's efforts to participate in the economic system: too often, government cronies, networks, and elite manipulation of the rules derail the most qualified.

Let me introduce you to Emad, a young man whom I met in Jordan. Emad's is the quintessential tale of a young Arab who is poor, educated, and dreams of a better life. Emad was raised by a single, illiterate mother in a farming community in northern Jordan. His father was a man already well into his sixties when Emad was born. Left an inheritance of small plots of land and seeing little prospect of social mobility locally, Emad's mother drilled a single message into her children's heads: "an education will secure you a prosperous future." Emad studied hard and scored well on national exams in his final year of secondary school. National examination systems, prevalent throughout the Middle East, often allow the poorest of young people to perform exceptionally well: success in such exams requires rote memorization, thus making dedication to study time a simple, though time-consuming, strategy to achieve high marks. The grades determine which university and department a student may attend. Final marks and students' names are made public, so that everyone knows each other's ranking, which ensures transparency, but does little to respect individual privacy. Emad's score got him accepted into an engineering program at Yarmouk University.

For all the warranted criticism that pedagogy in the Arab world does not encourage critical thinking skills, it is important to note that their education systems' dependence on national exams, widely practised in public schools across the region in the final year of high school, can provide a level playing field for citizens. Generally speaking, when one looks at the national rankings of many high school graduates in the Arab region, poorer communities can score as high as wealthier areas. Indeed, without doing well in the national exam, it is generally difficult even for someone from a family with wealth and political power to get into a public university, especially into a coveted discipline such as Emad's engineering. And despite the widespread growth of private universities in the region, public universities still command societal prestige. Emad was able to boast that his own hard work earned him a spot in a leading Jordanian university in a desirable discipline.

Throughout most of his time in Jordan's public education system, Emad was relatively sheltered from the ugly reality of his lower socio-economic class, lack of political power, and absence of a powerful network, or *wasta*, to get ahead. Yet, even though he received an entrance scholarship to university, Emad's costs of supplies and transportation were too high for an unemployed widow living in a farming community. Fortunately, Emad received financial support from his older half-brothers, and he was able to travel to the nearby city of Irbid to finish his education.

To be sure, many Arab countries – particularly Egypt – have not kept pace with investment in public schools, putting underserviced communities at a great disadvantage and making it impossible for those without the necessary means to, say, hire a tutor to attain a decent education. Moreover, as noted, many Arab youth, upon graduation, face the Herculean task of finding employment in a tight job market. Without a network or contacts in tribes, sects, or other communal groups, many young people like Emad remain unemployed or underemployed.

For Arab youth who feel they deserve better, this is a frustrating time. In conjunction with their political awakening online (discussed in the next chapter), a growing number of Arab youth are reacting to these challenging economic and social realities in the only way they see fit: by pulling up their bootstraps and going it alone.

The Rise of an Entrepreneurial Spirit

Increasing numbers of Arab youth today are creating and fostering a new and vibrant private sector of small businesses from the bottom up. Almost 3.6 million Egyptians are early entrepreneurs. They are mainly young men, live in Cairo, have a postsecondary degree, and are entering the retail, trade, and hospitality sectors to make ends meet.[28] In a survey of Arab youth in sixteen countries, many strongly believed they were more likely to be an entrepreneur than was their parents' generation.[29] And they are right. In a survey of attitudes about entrepreneurship in sixty-nine countries, youth in the Arab region overwhelmingly (83.1 per cent) agreed that "starting a business is considered a good career choice." In contrast, 70.9 per cent of those in all developing regions surveyed and only 63.0 per cent of those in European countries agreed.[30] In their confidence of having the "required knowledge or skills," Arab youth surpassed their counterparts all over the world except for sub-Saharan Africa.[31] Arab youth also believed more strongly than youth elsewhere that "persons growing a successful new business receive high status." In another survey, 15 per cent of respondents among Arab youth said they wanted to start their own business, while only 4 per cent of American youth shared this sentiment.[32] Of course, these cross-national survey results do not measure actuality, but they do measure youth perceptions and give a sense of their value system. Arab youth support the principle of the free market and generally respect the role and career path of an entrepreneur in society. Arab youth today are excited about entrepreneurship; in this, they stand apart from their counterparts elsewhere.

In meeting with youth across the Arab region, I encountered a more sombre tone when it came to the subject of finding the right job. Yet, rather than being resigned to their lot, they often said, "If I can't find the job I want, I will start my own business." There is a palpable mood in favour of finding business opportunities in everything. Many of the young people I met, from Morocco to the UAE, wanted to share their ideas about a possible business venture. A number of exciting regional initiatives are helping to propel this entrepreneurial spirit forward. Among them is Injaz, a regional initiative that provides mentoring and support for high school students who want to scale up their entrepreneurial ideas. Among other projects, Qatar-based Silatech is helping Moroccan banks offer savings accounts to youth, a noted impediment that young people face in getting credit and growing their businesses. Many of these regional initiatives are enabling multisectoral dialogue among public, private, and civil society actors to help young people succeed.

Perhaps my favourite regional initiative to spur creativity and innovation among Arab youth is *Stars of Science*, a popular televised competition sponsored by the Qatar Foundation in which youth develop, design, and test inventions in front of a panel of experts, while viewers vote for their favourite creation. Winners are awarded hundreds of thousands of dollars in prizes. By its sixth season, the show, which earns millions of YouTube views and Facebook "likes," had featured eighty contestants who collectively had filed more than sixty patents. The show's greatest success, however, is in helping Arab youth realize the great potential of their entrepreneurial spirit.[33]

I had the opportunity to speak at the Emirates Foundation for Youth Development, which uses an interesting model of social enterprise and venture philanthropy to promote leadership programs that empower young people to become entrepreneurs. At this forum, I met a dynamic group of young people who were optimistic about their future, and who wanted to learn more about how to scale up their ideas and get their products and services to wider markets. Among them was a notable number of young female entrepreneurs, a growing group in the Arab region. Shireen, for example, had started a centre for children with learning disabilities. Using her own funds and her own flair for arguing passionately for social change, Shireen has seen her centres grow into franchises that now make a profit. I asked her how and why she and so many women are becoming entrepreneurs. According to Shireen, "The Gulf is a competitive place now with so many talented people. Women here are getting a higher education to challenge themselves, to build their personalities, and to be able to become entrepreneurs in the future. With government support, providing positive leadership and promoting the idea that we can be leaders in our society, women are responding positively to all these opportunities." Amira, an Emirati woman who also leads an organization that helps young people pursue private sector opportunities, attributes successful female entrepreneurship in the Arab world to government initiatives such as providing licences allowing women to start businesses at home.

At the larger level of the economy, public sector employment continues to account for 60 to 80 per cent of the employed population in the Arab region,[34] but attitudinal surveys of young people show a drop in interest in working in the public sector and a rise in interest in the private sector. In 2012, 55 per cent of Arab youth surveyed wanted a public sector job; just two years later, this fig-ure stood at 43 per cent.[35] Most interestingly, perhaps, is the pro-nounced drop in the Gulf states, even though wages are higher in the public sector than in the private sector.

None of this is meant to ignore the presence of significant barri-ers to entrepreneurship in the region. Only a low number of uni-versity programs support studies in entrepreneurship or equity and finance issues such as micro-credit loans, red tape, and regula-tory barriers. There is also a pervasive culture of risk aversion and fear of failure.[36] Still, Arab youth are passionate about civic engage-ment and about finding solutions to everyday problems as entre-preneurs. One start-up filling a niche in online education, modelled on the success of the Khan Academy, is the Tahrir Academy, which provides free online content on a range of topics from "what causes migraines" to "advanced physics." Started by Egyptian expatriate Wael Ghonim – the man behind the infamous Facebook page "We are all Khaled Said," which criticized police brutality and helped ignite the 2011 revolution in Egypt – Tahrir Academy has uploaded more than a thousand educational videos for public consumption, many of them produced in Egypt, which have received more than four million views in less than two years.[37]

Growing entrepreneurship, however, is not an excuse for Arab governments to shirk their responsibility to implement policies that generate jobs. Too often, government and business leaders refer to entrepreneurship as a way to download the solution for job creation onto the private sector and legitimize government cut-backs and state retreat. As Mariana Mazzucato pointedly argues in her book, *The Entrepreneurial State*, this type of "discursive" tension is a myth. The role of government in promoting and sup-porting entrepreneurs can be traced through a broad spectrum of modern industries from hi-tech to pharmaceutical to green tech-nologies. The successful growth of many Western companies to-day is thanks to state policies and support. The lesson here is that Arab governments must continue to play a valuable role as en-gines of growth and inducers of innovative productivity.[38] Finally, entrepreneurship is not a panacea for youth unemployment, and governments must do more, particularly given the increase in unemployment since the Arab Spring, but the drive to forge ahead without looking to the state for employment is a huge attitudinal change among Arab youth, and lays the groundwork for a more confident generation.

Seizing the Demographic Dividend

What will help these entrepreneurs and other young Arabs succeed? A youthful society creates a natural, self-sustaining consumer market and innovative labour pool. Throughout the Arab world, the number of the very young, those up to age fourteen, is shrinking and the number age sixty-five and older is growing negligibly, while those in the economically productive years between twenty-five and sixty-four are expanding. The average Arab household thus will soon shift from one full of dependants to one full of working-age individuals. Lower dependency ratios and rising human capital could produce rapid economic growth that might be sustained for at least a generation. This is the demographic dividend – or demographic gift, as some have called it – that the Arab region will soon enjoy.

In contrast, North America, Europe, Japan, and even China (until it fully relaxes its one-child policy) face a future of high dependency ratios – of households with fewer and fewer working-age people and more and more elderly dependants. This is not just a problem for pension systems; it is also a diversion of domestic savings from investments to public consumption in the form of social security payments and health services. It is also adding to the burden placed on the declining proportion of working-age adults and to the taxes they pay. Another challenge for aging populations is the slowdown in productivity and innovation: whether one means productivity of manufacturing processes or innovation in product design and service delivery, aging societies are less likely to produce and innovate with the same speed and advantage as younger societies. This is the upside of an educated, consumer-savvy, eager, and confident youth bulge.

There is a reason marketing firms spend a great deal of money trying to capture the brand loyalty of younger people: they are the future consumer base that can make or break a product. Youthful societies are naturally a more promising consumer market for goods and services than are aging societies, where downsizing is more frequent and pronounced. Those geared to the increasing number of elderly aside, most goods and services in our age of capitalism and hyper-consumerism are aimed at providing what youthful societies "want," not necessarily what they "need." For demographers this explains why we will continue to see economic growth shift towards the relatively more youthful emerging market economies in the Arab region and elsewhere.

A large, youthful population is a natural market for global goods and services as well, yet viewing the Arab Middle East as a region of untapped consumers has not always been easy for businesses. In *The Arab World Unbound: Tapping into the Power of 350 Million Consumers*, marketing professor Vijay Mahajan argues, however, that the Arab region is a flourishing marketplace ripe with business opportunities. Not only does the Arab Middle East have a huge consumer market, as indicated in the book's subtitle, but the region ranks as the world's ninth-largest economy in terms of its aggregate GDP. Mahajan says that the apprehension of global businesses about operating in the Middle East is reminiscent of what he heard in the 1990s when businesses wanted to ignore the BRICS (Brazil, Russia, India, China, South Africa) as potential markets because they were "relatively modest, complex, and easily ignored."[39] The Arab world's demographics mean, however, that global companies cannot long ignore it or its importance for future world economic growth.

Will the Arab world become just another dumping ground for Western brands manufactured in East Asia? I think not. To explain, let me introduce you to Fulla, who, according to her website, "is sixteen years old. She's Arab, body and soul. She loves life and learning. She honours her parents and loves her family and friends." She's also going to take out Barbie – yes, Fulla is a doll, conceived in the heart of the Middle East. After a few months in the Middle

East in the mid-2000s with my then young daughter, "pester power" – a term coined by marketing gurus and typically embodied by children who, like my daughter, watch a seemingly endless amount of local TV – worked its magic on me. We made our way to Mecca Mall, where I bought my daughter a Fulla doll, complete with car, hairbrush, and all of the necessary accessories. Unlike Barbie, however, Fulla represents Muslim values – for example, she occasionally dons a fashionable *hijab* as part of the "Fulla haute couture collection," and bikinis, short skirts, or, needless to say, a Ken-like male companion doll were not "sold separately." If you could bank on one of two companies, Mattel's Barbie or NewBoy Design's Fulla, which is likely to be more successful in twenty years' time? Chances are the aging West will buy fewer Barbies and the Middle East more Fullas.

To take another example, my son – like so many kids in the Middle East – is addicted to video games. In fact, the region has one of the fastest-growing communities of online gamers in the world, and demographics mean this is likely to remain true for many years to come. Capitalizing on this growth industry, Semanoor, a Saudi firm, invented Faris, a new hero for the Arab world's online gaming industry. As a character in the video game *Unearthed: Trail of Ibn Battuta*, Faris "embarks on an exotic adventure throughout the Middle East on the trail of the famous Muslim explorer Ibn Battuta. The trail won't be clear however as Faris and his archeologist sister Dania [who wears a *hijab*] will have to overcome an unholy alliance of a militia army leader, a weapons dealer and a wealthy antiquities smuggler who are after the same goal."[40] Faris provides a positive Arab hero in a gaming community that too often depicts Arabs as terrorists. *Unearthed* is the first major Arabic-language video game launched on Sony PlayStation 3, and it has been redeveloped for iPad and Android devices, ready for consumers searching for a new vision of Arabs in the online world. More recently, it was announced that the latest instalment of the phenomenally popular *Tekken* series, *Tekken 7*, will feature several new characters, including Shaheen, "a cool Arab fighter" as described by *Tekken* director Katushiro Harada. Sporting a traditional *keffiyeh* headscarf and a flowing cape and coat, Shaheen was developed in response to players' demand for a strong, non-stereotypical Arab character. The design of the Shaheen character received much player feedback during its initial stages and, "buoyed by the design's positive response, Harada pursued the Arabic design, with Shaheen becoming the first Saudi Arabian character to appear in the Tekken series – usually dominated by Western and Asian character builds."[41]

The Fulla, Faris, and now Shaheen characters remind us that the Arab region's cultural uniqueness and diversity are no barriers to business; instead, they are an opportunity to create new products and services. The engine of economic growth is shifting to the emerging market economies, and for businesses that succeed, the profits will come not from the labour of physical production but from innovation, services, and marketing. Although many emerging market economies are trying to grow by becoming assembly plants, the Arab region will harness its internal market, expand its intellectual capital to become a global leader in services provision, and invest regionally. Here, Arab youth are key to the region's success.

Fulla, Faris, and Shaheen are also examples of how Arab youth are creating their own identities, rather than sticking to the binary of Islam versus Modernism – a subject I return to in Chapter 4 – as if the two are mutually exclusive. Arab youth are customizing their consumption choices to suit their beliefs and customs. This is a source for economic potential: again, in the life cycle of a product, the manufacturing process is not where the added value is introduced. Conception, design, marketing, and brand management require local knowledge, so a Western or Western-like product still needs the innovation of an Arab workforce to adapt, accommodate, and market it in the Arab region, a process that "localizes" products and services. Before the Arab Spring, autocratic governments stunted the ambitions of Arab youth; now, they have a new-found sense of economic empowerment that cannot be quelled. Not only are young Arabs demanding more of their governments, they are poised to share their intelligence, ingenuity, and creativity.

The Arab region's demographic dividend offers a consumer market brimming with economic potential, but I believe an Arab "creative class" could benefit the most. Richard Florida, in *The Rise of the Creative Class*, first introduced and propelled the concept of how creative people in technology, journalism, entertainment, finance, marketing, and the arts are courted by cities that offer a hip, vibrant, and diverse space for work, play, and leisure.[42] In essence, cosmopolitan people are attracted to work in cities that have character and an atmosphere that fosters their particular sensibility. It is worth understanding the importance of these creative individuals – problem solvers who are usually university educated, young, and globally connected – for the success of many world-class cities, including in the Arab world. Creativity, not a plethora of unskilled labour, will underscore the future growth of the world economy.

It is often stated that the Arab world missed the manufacturing revolution by not competing with Southeast Asia or parts of Latin America to capture the benefits of globalization in goods trade. This might have been the case, particularly for more populous countries such as Egypt, but few Arab countries want to participate in a race to the bottom to compete on the basis of low-skilled labour. There is a better development model. The Arab world has an opportunity to take advantage of its educated youth, a strong internal consumer market, and the potential of a growing creative class to play a key role in the global economy. Indeed, the Arab world is ripe with young people who have the "soft skills" that global companies and employers want and need. Arab universities have been criticized for turning out too many humanities and social science graduates (63 per cent) and too few science graduates (28 per cent),[43] but such criticism is short-sighted: it is out of the former disciplines that the majority of a creative class will emerge. Many of the nearly 25 per cent who graduated in business and the social sciences in 2008[44] will capitalize on the energies of a creative culture and help propel their countries towards greater economic growth.

This is not to say that Arab cities have already definitively produced a creative class. In my view, however, it is coming. The missing element is freedom to think outside the box. The value of a liberal arts degree is in the skills it teaches to assess a situation critically and to use the communicative tools of writing, debating, and speaking to find creative employment. The decade preceding the

Arab Spring saw the beginning of this societal questioning, and the coming decades will see Arab youth leveraging their postsecondary education to add value to the global economy. Already, cities such as Casablanca, Tunis, Dubai, Amman, Beirut, and Doha are on the path to becoming places conducive to the growth of a creative class, but they need the insight of progressive urban planners and political leaders to succeed. Like many cities elsewhere in the world that have attracted, retained, and taken full advantage of a creative class, Arab cities need to satisfy the socio-cultural demands and needs of creative people. This might mean increased access to festivals, public spaces, galleries, universities, and social activities, the availability of plug-and-play communities, interesting cafés, business hubs and incubators, and a community welcoming of cosmopolitan young people.[45] Already, the visitor to Dubai cannot help but feel the creative buzz of its young, cosmopolitan workforce, one that draws in people from all over the world. Indeed, when surveyed, Arab youth overwhelmingly voice a desire to live in the UAE, rather than in the United States, France, or other Western states.[46] Beirut's charm and art scene continue to entice people to live and work there despite its political challenges. Cairo and Amman thrive on the charm of neighbourhoods – such as Mohandiseen and Jabal Wabdeh – full of unique character, authenticity, and artistic flair. By 2050, almost three-quarters of the Arab region will be urban, another key requisite for fostering a creative class unshackled by such values as clan, sect, and pedigree. This development is also promising for the creation of economies of scale as urban areas also spark consumption and innovation.

Conclusion

The Arab region has witnessed the diminishing role of the state over the past twenty years, a transition that has changed the way youth look at and think about the role of government in economic affairs. Arab governments can no longer afford to be the engine of growth; instead, they increasingly depend on the private sector to create, innovate, and produce. Arab youth have no strong memory of the paternalistic state, and are willing to compete in the global marketplace. In Cairo, I met a number of university students who were willing to work as interns in Western companies to build their resumés after graduation. A decade ago, the concept of working for free in a private company, for up to six months at a time, was simply unheard of; today, Cairo youth compete for unpaid internships to strengthen their qualifications and gain valuable skills. Postsecondary education has become a must for men and women alike, in both rural and urban areas. These young, educated Arabs will deliver a demographic dividend for the entire region.

One can see the creative juices of young Arab people at work in their willingness to open their own businesses, court venture capitalists, seek out markets for their products and services, and actively participate in the global marketplace. As one young man from Jordan told me, "As soon as I can borrow a small sum of money, I'll open a roadside café and serve treats and drinks. At least this will help generate my spending money and from there I'll open another and another. I won't abandon my dreams to enter a digital marketing firm, but there's profit wherever one searches for it in Jordan."

From roadside cafés to the online world, Arab youth are finding new economic opportunities that did not exist before. Online opportunities are flourishing to create applications that meet the needs of young Arabs, from apps to avoid Cairo's notorious traffic jams to directory services to help Amman residents find doctors, barbers, and government offices. This kind of entrepreneurial spirit and creative thinking springs from the power of digital technology. From social media to online shopping, digital technology is allowing people to find investors and markets worldwide. Moreover, as the Internet and telecommunications become privatized across the region, governments will have less control over what the future of entrepreneurship looks like. There are still challenges, particularly with access to financing, but young Arabs' attitudes about work and productivity are changing, especially in urban areas. Young people no longer depend on the state for employment or consider education merely a process to attain employment. Rather, they now see education as an end in itself. Women, in particular, have high expectations of attaining postsecondary education as a means to build their confidence and prepare themselves for the future, whether as the head of a boardroom or the head of a household.

When Arab youth are asked to choose from a long list of challenges facing the Middle East, their greatest concern by far is the rising cost of living, followed by the national economy and government corruption. Issues that we in the West would identify as the most significant "Middle East challenges" – militarization, press freedom, the right to vote – are on the bottom rung of Arab youth's concerns. Bread before freedom and dignity was the priority for those youth shouting in Tahrir Square and beyond. One should not misconstrue this preference, however, as justification for political oppression and authoritarianism. As I highlight in the next chapter, Arab youth want political freedom and are working creatively to attain political accountability and reform.

chapter three

Freedom

Economic woes were an important impetus behind the Arab Spring, but one cannot divorce these concerns from the political situation many Arabs face. The way Arab youth perceive the role of government has fundamentally changed from how their parents' generation understood the social contract.

For decades after Arab states secured their independence from colonial powers, and during the height of the Cold War between the world's superpowers, the Arab region was home to some of the most closed political systems in the world. Acquiescence to political leaders was necessary to build modern states from the top down – at least, this was what Arabs were told in last half of the twentieth century. Today's generation of Arab youth does not value deference. They have been told, and have internalized, the idea that the state will be modernized from the bottom up.

Arab governments and leaders come in many different types, ranging from iron-fisted dictatorships like that of Syria's Bashar al-Assad to dysfunctional, quasi-liberal democracies such as Lebanon, the Palestinian territories, and Iraq to monarchies – some, like Morocco under King Mohammed VI, ruled by progressive liberals, and others, like Saudi Arabia under King Salman, socially conservative theocracies. Given the democratic waves that swept Latin America, eastern Europe, and many parts of Asia in the 1980s, it seemed as though the Middle East would be the last region to open up its political system to more democratic rule.

Yet, as out of touch with the rest of the world and with the needs of the people as many Arab governments seem to be, so are behaviouralist theories that blame socio-cultural factors for slow political or economic development. Applied to the region, these theories argue that Arab culture – and, implicitly, the religion of Islam – is somehow antithetical to democracy. The prevalence of these theories, in turn, has led many Western analysts, in a blind fit of cultural reductionist argument, to talk of "Arab exceptionalism," of the Arab region as a holdout against globalization, democracy, and modernity. Often, the blame is placed on Arabs themselves, who are characterized as apathetic, indifferent, or even apolitical. Sadly, some – including political and economic elites who stand to gain from the status quo – still argue that Arabs are not "ready" for democracy. Academics, too, often describe how "authoritarian resilience" has institutionalized its presence in the Arab region,[1] as they overlook the signs of economic, political, and social change. Some refer to the "regional permeability" of the Arab world, where external pressures to democratize, changing internal discourse about human rights, and the rising power of civil society are slowly changing autocratic systems from within.[2] Few, however, foresaw the Arab Spring or the changing political discourse that generational change has brought about in the Middle East.

In this chapter, I want to show that, below the surface, beyond the academic focus on political parties and civil society organizations, a generation of Arabs is talking and thinking about politics in fundamentally different ways than did their elders. The slogan of Arab youth is freedom – freedom from the rampant corruption and oppression that prevents them from pursuing social, political, and economic opportunities to the fullest of their potential. The technological changes that have swept the Arab world have allowed youth to crystallize their views about freedom from corruption, nepotism, and discrimination. Online media allow youth to absorb and generate new ideas about how things ought to be in the relationship between government and the people, and about the capacity of youth to challenge state inadequacies. It is difficult to measure this change in political discourse, but few who visit and live in the Arab region could ignore the tectonic shifts in the attitudes of Arab youth. One need only look back before the Arab awakening to see how the opening of the floodgates of information has empowered Arab youth to call for freedom.

Before the Arab Awakening

For decades Arab governments brooked no criticism of their rule. With strong government control over the security sectors of police, intelligence, and the army, political opposition was kept at bay through fear and repression. Freedom of speech and assembly more often than not were curtailed. Few means existed to ensure accountability, voice dissent, or challenge political structures. Information and media were centralized under state control, from government newspapers that never spoke ill of the almighty leader to state-owned television stations that showed only glorious national accomplishments.

Today Arab youth have access to hundreds of popular free-to-air programming satellite television channels – many of which stream news highly critical of Arab governments and international affairs – endless online information resources, mobile applications that circumvent government services, and plenty of social media platforms to challenge their governments and call for accountability. Arab youth are nimble online, proving again and again that they are able to challenge censorship, voice their opinions, and outwit the electronic armies sent by the authorities to capture their avatars. Beginning online and slowly traversing to offline spaces, youth are creating new communities of shared political views and hopes. Generally, these have not yet matured into institutionalized political parties or ideological groupings – the kinds of entities political scientists might seek out in their efforts to find and document budding liberal democracies. Yet the political givens of the past decades of Arab history – accepting strongman rule in exchange for stability, not questioning the use of the public purse, indifference towards elements of a liberal democracy – were seriously undermined by the Arab Spring. The provocateurs who truly pushed the questioning of these political givens were Arab youth, who could not accept the status quo because it no longer – if it ever did – matched their social reality, in part thanks to globalization, rising education levels, and an increasing spirit of independence and initiative.

One political given the Arab Spring shattered was the long-abused and outdated idea of the indispensability of the strongman leader and his role as harbinger of stability. Although no Arab country descended to the levels of cultish propaganda one sees in totalitarian North Korea, where people weep for love of and devotion to a supreme leader, some came close. Leaders such as Muammar Gaddafi, Hafez al-Assad, and Saddam Hussein were exceptionally aggressive in imposing their own cult of personality. These one-man-rule governments created a security apparatus and social narrative best described as "a republic of fear."[3] The political purpose of such a system was to create an allure of legitimacy surrounding the unelected political leader, who controlled a relatively new state with no historical reference point, and to keep dissent at bay.

The "republic of fear" was not the norm in the region, but Arab leaders nevertheless placed great emphasis on the need for stability through upholding the status quo. When Arab states gained independence from colonial powers – Britain, France, and Italy – their names often did not exist on the political map. Many were made-up constructs to most of their inhabitants. For centuries, identity had been formed along tribes, families, religious sects, classes, occupations, and cities or towns. Arabs did not identify themselves, for example, as Iraqi, Lebanese, or Libyan. Much as their former colonial masters did, the new ruling elites had to persuade the inhabitants to identify themselves as citizens of these newly demarcated states. This was not always an easy task, since identities often crossed borders: people with shared identities effectively had been separated by the strokes of colonialists' pens. The new Arab states, therefore, needed to build a nation-state of citizens who did not question the legitimacy of the new borders. Consequently, they evoked or invented national symbols and imagery, national militaries, stories of national heroism, and, of course, the indispensability of new state leaders – and a police and security apparatus to hold it all together.

There are countless examples of how this strongman propaganda prevailed in the Arab region, but let me share a few of my own experiences that remain particularly memorable. During visits to Syria in the mid-1980s was when I first saw the Orwellian propaganda that some states used to keep people in check. Images of then-president Hafez al-Assad were everywhere – as statues in the middle of roundabouts, plastered on banners over every government building and on street billboards, framed photographs in every shop and restaurant, posters taped onto the back windows of cars, taxis, and buses. His expression in these portraits was invariably stern. Dressed in military attire, Assad was seen peering off into the distance as though omnipotent. The message was that Assad was a father figure – *baba* Hafez – whose most important task was to protect his people. External threats – the Israelis, the West, foreign infiltrators – meant that Syria needed a man like Assad to keep from being enslaved.

With only a few radio frequencies and television stations with terrestrial antennae available, people depended on local, state-controlled programming. The theme was always the same: news about what Assad was doing that day, whom he met, what decisions were enacted, and what awards he was bequeathing on allies. Of course, these did not include personal interviews with Assad – just narrated stories of his day-to-day activities that presented him as commander-in-chief at all times. The newscast was typically followed by a musical break, during which a relatively unknown singer would praise Assad as defender of the country. During the song, images of Syria's historical and cultural icons would flash across the screen, intermixed with military parades, Assad in sunglasses, and, occasionally, a glimpse of the soft side of *baba* Hafez with a young child. These music videos would play throughout the day between state television programming of soap operas, films, and Western (usually subtitled) reruns. Assad was rarely presented as a family man, in social company, pictured in his home, or dressed in casual wear. There was no mistaking the imagery or the heroism, nationalism, and strength that Assad was meant to embody.

In one sense the deliberate effort to create nation-states among the Arabs worked. Few Arabs today question the legitimacy of state borders – indeed, many identify as citizens of these states. Current discussion by so-called pundits about "the end of the Sykes-Picot" borders is an exaggeration.[4] Of course, many non-Arab minorities – including Kurds, Berbers, and Assyrians – continue to seek self-determination or autonomy; other peoples – Palestinians, Bedoon of the Gulf, Western Saharans – remain stateless and have serious objections to colonial demarcations and state annexations. On the whole, however, Arabs today are proud of their state identities, and see themselves as Algerians, Libyans, Syrians, Omanis, Kuwaitis, and so on. The territories colonial rulers constructed have become cemented identities in the minds of most Arabs throughout the Middle East and North Africa, even though such identities originated in the propaganda of securitization and rallying around the flag in defence of an external enemy.

Like the national identity, the social contract in many Arab countries was premised on the notion that the leader, much like Hobbes's *Leviathan*, would provide security and stability; in exchange, the people would give up their political rights and freedoms. To ensure that the people acquiesced in this bargain, a heavy-handed security and intelligence apparatus kept a watchful eye on anyone who questioned the leader's legitimacy and indispensability and, implicitly, the sanctity of the state. I do not believe the Syrian people of the 1980s ever truly accepted Hafez al-Assad's strongman rule as a given. In fact, many of the people I knew paid a heavy price for having family and friends who defied his authority. Fear was palpable in Syria and among Syrians. Parents did not dare to talk politics in front of their children, who might report to their teachers the next day about "suspicious and subversive" activity. The "walls had ears," I was often told.

In 1982 the city of Hama, in the middle of the Syrian heartland, was the site of one of the worst massacres of civilians and political opponents in the entire Arab world. Stopping in Hama on my way from Damascus to Aleppo was a type of homage I will never forget. As I stood in front of Hama's historic and iconic water wheels in 1987, I felt the chill and horror of what had happened only five years before. With my Auntie Sana from Canada, I stood by the water wheels in silence for a long time. After saying a small prayer, and with my auntie weeping quietly, we left the city behind. Only when we had left Syrian soil did Auntie Sana dare to describe the horrors her family had endured here.

Assad's army entered Hama to quash an uprising of political opponents, many belonging to the Muslim Brotherhood movement, but the crackdown soon widened to include any male of potential fighting age. The story is told that men were beckoned to the mosques and gunned down inside. Soldiers then went from house to house for twenty-seven days, killing anyone who might be an opponent of Assad. The death toll is unknown, but estimates range from 10,000 to 40,000. My auntie later recalled that women in this mostly conservative Muslim city stopped wearing the *hijab* simply because there were no men left in the city for whom women needed to be modestly dressed. An entire generation was without young men. My auntie lost male cousins and has never forgotten the horror of Hama. Because of these experiences relayed to me, I will never forget it, either.

When political opponents questioned Assad's legitimacy, the narrative his regime quickly adopted was that these individuals were trying to undermine the state – that they were, in fact, terrorists who needed to be quashed by military might. With no such thing as the Internet or cell phones, barely any landline telephones, and little in the way of citizen reporting, the events of Hama were scarcely known outside sanctioned government channels. The slaughter came to light only gradually, through word of mouth, particularly among members of the Syrian diaspora, making its way into Western media sources.

It is no coincidence that the same language, slogans, and other tactics that Hafez al-Assad used in 1982 were appropriated by his son Bashar during the uprisings that began in 2011. This time, however, the people, many of whom had lost loved ones to the brutal Assad regime, refused to be silent. The campaign, overwhelmingly youth driven, to expose the nature of the regime gave rise to citizen journalists and activists who demanded freedom.

Opening the Floodgates of Ideas

The Arab awakening in Syria during the spring of 2011 had its roots in the rural town of Daraa, where families protested the torture of children who had written anti-regime slogans on a school chalk-board. It was university students in Damascus, however, who galvanized a nationwide movement against the killing and mutilation by security forces of twelve-year-old Hamza Ali Al-Khateeb, whose only crime was demonstrating against the torture of Daraa's children. The university students – whose parents were often members of the merchant economic class with economic means – were incensed by the violence and brutality of the Assad regime, and could not fathom that any government had the legitimacy or authority to treat children in this horrific way.

What a difference there was between the 1982 and 2011 uprisings in Syria. In 1982 few reports of the Assad regime's horrors left the city, few lists of names were ever published, and, fearful of the state security apparatus, few Syrians – even in the diaspora – dared tell their stories publicly. In 2011 gruesome pictures of Hamza's mutilated corpse were shared across the globe. The same university students who took to flash mob protests in Damascus also took to the Internet to expose Assad's crimes. Less than a month after Hamza's death, a Facebook page dedicated to him had attracted more than 100,000 followers; three years later the number had risen to 759,000. His image was shared on cell phones across the region, and few Arabs can say that they have not seen those horrible images. Sadly, Hamza is now just one of tens of thousands of children killed in the Syrian conflict, but he sparked a movement by Syrian youth who simply would not ignore the brutality of the Assad regime.

Throughout the Arab region, decades of state-controlled information had been a powerful means to ensure political submission and to shape public perceptions and opinions in favour of the elite few. Multiple surveys of Arab people have found that they continue to receive their primary information from television. Yet the landscape of televised programming has changed drastically since the mid-1990s. Today just over half of all Arab households watch TV using a satellite receiver, giving them access to over seven hundred free-to-air channels, mostly in Arabic, 76 per cent of them privately owned.[5] Print and radio are primarily of local origin, but television, the Internet, and social media are a mix of international and local sources[6] – indeed, as global media move away from print and radio and towards online sources, the Arab media landscape is becoming internationalized.

Although general-interest programming is the largest genre of satellite channel type, news and current affairs make up the second-largest category, and here one cannot ignore the influence of Qatar-based Al-Jazeera, which was the first news channel in the region not controlled by government. For the first time, Arab audiences were able to watch critical news about international affairs, their country, and region from a professional journalistic source – images and stories that did not paint their leaders in the glowing light of state media. Al-Jazeera exposed corruption and duplicity, and provided analysis that did not hold back for fear of state reprisal. Significantly, Al-Jazeera took a humanist approach to its programming by focusing on the perils faced by the average Arab, whether it was covering the devastating effects of war or the negative effects of government socio-economic policies. The quality and impartiality of Al-Jazeera Arabic has deteriorated over the years – especially through the Arab Spring, Al-Jazeera appeared to become increasingly beholden to the Qatari foreign policy narrative – but competitors have now arisen that offer a new narrative of equal criticism of government, raising the bar on providing more exposés and alternative analyses. These include outlets such as Al-Arabia, Al-Alam, Al-Manar, and Future News, to name a few. International news outlets such the BBC, France24, CNBC, DW, SkyTV, and Euronews have also begun to offer excellent Arabic news sister channels.

One of the most interesting contributions to news and current affairs programming in the Arab region is the rise of political talk shows and political satire shows. One that stood out for its impact during the Arab Spring is *El-Bernameg*. Hosted by Bassem Youssef, the show was modelled along the lines of Jon Stewart's *The Daily*

Show. On the heels of the 2011 Egyptian Revolution, the then thirty-seven-year-old Youssef took his already popular YouTube video program to television, where it became the most popular show in the Arab region. Youssef poked fun at political leaders, exposed government failures, ridiculed regional affairs, mocked the region's unprofessional media, and openly criticized Egyptian officials. The weekly television show quickly gained nearly thirty million viewers in Egypt alone, but it was youth – in Egypt and elsewhere – who were drawn most strongly to Youssef's sense of humour and sarcasm. The controversial show faced a number of hurdles in securing a channel willing to host it since the military returned to power in 2013 and, refusing to bow to political pressure, Youssef suspended the show in mid-2014. Although *El-Bernameg* is no longer on the air, it is hard to imagine that this style of programming will disappear completely now that the door has been opened. In the final chapter, I address the contention that the Arab Spring was a temporary phenomenon, and argue that, on the contrary, it is only the beginning.

Although many Arab governments have long succeeded in censoring print newspapers, state censorship is becoming increasingly difficult in the online age, and plenty of publications are testing the waters. As far back as the 1990s, a now-out-of-print publication called the *Cairo Times* went online to give readers a glimpse of what Egypt's censors deemed to be sensitive national material by highlighting text that the censors did not allow them to publish in print. News bits that noted government corruption or criticized President Hosni Mubarak or Egypt's peace treaty with Israel were almost always among the items highlighted. The *Cairo Times* case is a reminder that online sources can shine a light into the dark corners of state censorship and put pressure on governments to liberalize print media space or risk scandal, or at the very least embarrassment, once citizens know the facts.

Freedom of the press is often deemed to be a cornerstone of liberal democracy. For academics and citizens alike, one marker of political liberalization has been the ability of citizens to challenge and question their governments. Many Arab governments have yet to liberalize this space for absolute freedom of speech, but they are finding it more difficult to control the narrative. With the rise of online portals posting critical articles, the Arab region's print newspapers, now facing increased competition from the online world, have also modestly improved their critical content. This has given rise to independent newspapers throughout the region. In Egypt, for example, *Al-Masry Al-Youm* and *Al-Dustur* were founded in 2004 and 2007, respectively. English-language dailies, including Lebanon's *Daily Star* and the UAE's *The National*, have also improved the overall environment of journalism in the Middle East.

As the ecosystem of media has improved throughout the Arab region, Arab youth are also shifting their consumption of media from conventional sources (print, television) to online sources. The mixed way they now consume news and information shows that they are developing valuable critical thinking skills. The ability to access and traverse different media is an important part of creating critical thinking because it requires one to question and verify information that might be false. Every day, 67 per cent of Arab youth spend less than half an hour reading print media, 60 per cent spend less than three hours watching TV, but 70 per cent spend more than three hours online.[7] The turn to online platforms to access critical information or to express political frustrations is a growing phenomenon in the Arab region, and one that cannot be rolled back. This change in consumption is valuable not only because of the ease and feasibility of accessing information online, but also because the nature of this interaction and engagement with news and information allows youth to foster their own political conversations. Unlike traditional media based solely on youth consumption, online media allow youth to discuss and examine the political possibilities available to them.

Arab youth have a strong desire for freedom of speech. In a survey of three thousand youth in nine countries, 63 per cent said they wanted more freedom "to do and say what they want as long as it does not harm others"; these sentiments were highest in North Africa, then the Levant, and lastly in the Gulf.[8] More to the point, Arab youth now actively generate information both on and offline, which is having a profound socio-cultural and socio-political impact.[9] Take the case of Saudi Arabia, which has some of the strictest laws on press freedom in the world, but where many have turned to YouTube to voice their political views. Some of the videos young Saudis have uploaded have attracted more than two million views and continue to go viral in a country of twenty-eight million. In addition to entertainment and education, a common theme of these videos is self-expression and a growing demand for political and economic accountability.

Increasingly, Arab youth are using online forums to compensate for the restrictions they face in the offline world. They are already well connected, with access to information on satellite TV, online, and through their mobile phones. Indeed, the Middle East is one of the leading purchasers of mobile devices, second only to the highly populated Asia-Pacific region, and prices for mobile units continue to drop rapidly, giving greater access to more people. In 2011, over 80 per cent of the Arab population – and 87 per cent of Arab youth – had access to a mobile phone, with almost all regions covered by 3G technologies and many on the cusp of adopting 4G technologies.[10] Mobile phones are giving youth the opportunity to test social norms and conventions – some of which I look at in the next chapter – and are also being used as a tool for political mobilization when sharing experiences and grievances. Many of the mobile text messages sent during the Egyptian Revolution of January 2011 were of a highly political nature, including those that designated meeting areas for protestors, warnings about the location of police and security forces, and political messages of concerted demands. Throughout the Arab Spring, texts were used to create what Howard Rheingold describes as "smart mobs": "people who are able to act in concert even if they don't know each other ... [and to] cooperate in ways never before possible."[11] Mobile phones have given rise to freedoms that would have been inconceivable by previous generations, and general access to smartphone technology will only make these freedoms more widespread. Smartphones have already become the mobile technology used by the majority of Qataris, Emiratis, Saudis, and Jordanians. In Egypt, the largest Arab country, 25 per cent of the population has a smartphone. Moreover, 72 per cent of all smartphone owners are under age thirty-four.[12] It is projected that, by 2020, nearly 50 per cent of all Arabs will have a smartphone that could cost less than US$50.[13]

Although the Arab region's smartphone penetration is still in its early stages, there has already been a remarkable growth in online connectivity among Arab youth: in the survey of Arab youth in nine countries referred to above, 83 per cent of respondents said they access the Internet daily, and 76 per cent do so from home.[14] It is estimated that, in 2014, nearly 13 million Arab youth were actively engaging online.[15] Most important, the rate of connectivity is growing faster in the Arab region than in the rest of the world, thanks to improved investment into telecommunications infrastructure, increased competition among private service providers, and a strong demand by Arab youth to go online: Arab Internet users grew by 23 per cent each year from 2006 to 2011, while most of the rest of the world increased by 14 per cent.[16] Broadband speed is also increasing rapidly in the Arab region, by 20 per cent from 2011 to 2012 alone. In 2013, 90 million people in the Arab region (40.2 per cent of the population) were connected to the Internet, a number that is expected to grow to 413 million in 2015.[17] It is estimated, that in 2014, nearly 13 million Arab youth were actively engaging online.

Arab youth are social-media savvy, using platforms such as Facebook and, to a lesser extent, Twitter and LinkedIn. On average, Arab youth spend one to three hours a day socializing on these sites.[18] In 2013, the Arab region had seven million Twitter users, and no fewer than sixty-two million active Facebook users, forty-two million of whom accessed the site on their mobile phone. Indeed, after television, Facebook is the most important source of information for Arab viewers,[19] and it remains a powerful, uncensored portal for news consumption as well. News stories and articles are shared online, creating a discourse that is generated from the bottom up, not monopolized by government minders.

Short online videos like those found on YouTube have also become increasingly popular among Arab youth. The Arab region is among the highest consumers of YouTube videos in the world, with 34 per cent in the UAE and 30 per cent in Egypt using the site daily. Saudi Arabia has the highest download rate of YouTube videos in the world: 42 per cent of Saudi youth watch YouTube videos every day, three times the proportion in the United States and far more than in the United Kingdom and France (15 per cent each) or Germany (12 per cent).[20] Every day, a hundred million YouTube videos are watched in the Arab world, and every minute Arabs upload an hour of YouTube video content – all in a forum free of government controls and official censorship.[21]

Youth-Generated Content

After decades of a dominant state-led narrative created through censorship of media and political expression, the floodgates of free access to information have opened in the Arab world. In this new space, Arabs – Arab youth, in particular – have become increasingly empowered as they realize their ability to shake their governments' *raison d'être* as self-proclaimed guardians of stability. Moreover, Arab youth have become disenchanted with the notion that their governments' abuse of political and economic power has been worth the maintenance of the status quo. Widespread government corruption remains a deep concern for Arab youth, many of whom now doubt the capability of their governments to meet their economic, political, and social expectations.

Moreover, Arab youth's connectivity in an age of increased information flows is permitting them to engage in new conversations about their governments' failings. Marc Lynch, notably in *Voices of the New Arab Public* and *The Arab Uprising*, captures the essence of this new information flow and its relationship with the Arab people in his concept of the "new Arab public sphere." Playing on political philosopher Jurgen Habermas's concept of the public sphere – an arena where citizens come together to discuss and debate sociopolitical concerns freely in order to achieve a consensus – Lynch identifies the way Arabs have carved out this space in the cybersphere. According to Lynch, as youth expressed their frustration with government, they became empowered with new technological tools of group and self-expression, and protested state control in the new Arab public sphere with relative reprieve from their countries' intelligence and security services. Lynch contends that the Arab uprisings were the beginning of a regional transformation, which continues to evolve and outpace government reforms. Furthermore, he notes that "the new public sphere relentlessly hunts down information about ... [state] transgressions and spreads it through all channels to hold the regimes accountable."[22]

For Arab youth, debating, demonstrating, and vocalizing their concerns with government institutions and policies in cyberspace has also had a positive spillover into offline public spaces and general discourse. Again, Arab youth are not just passive consumers of information, but agents in promoting and providing information with inherent social and political value that is changing public discourse away from the gatekeepers who previously dominated information generation and control in the Arab region. The heightened connectivity of Arab youth to web-related forums has given them an affordable and accessible tool with which to create and disseminate information that is profoundly reshaping their societies. By challenging state authorities via the Internet and social media, they are demanding a new social contract between citizens and government.

Bloggers in the Arab region first took to the Internet in the mid-1990s, but since the early 2000s blogs have been growing steadily, and Arabs are increasingly consuming and contributing to the blogosphere with provocative and insightful commentary on political life in the region. According to a Harvard University study, there were approximately thirty-five thousand Arabic blogs online in 2009. The study looked at nearly six thousand of these to assess their impact on public discourse. The topics most covered included personal reflections about life and national politics and news, with a notable criticism of political leaders. Other topics covered included religious issues, human rights, and cultural issues. Not surprisingly, most of the bloggers were young: 75 per cent were under age thirty-five. Bloggers also used their own names, and did not try to hide from their country's security service. Most were in Egypt, the most populous country in the region, while other large clusters were in Saudi Arabia and Kuwait.

Sixty per cent of all the bloggers in the region were men, but half of the bloggers in Egypt were women, as were 42 per cent of the bloggers in Saudi Arabia – a higher proportion than in the rest of the region.[23]

Many of the early bloggers harkened from the small liberal elite, and were young, left-leaning secularists who also wrote in English about the region.[24] A number of these English-language blogs about the Arab world, including Egypt's *Sandmonkey* and *Arabist*, Jordan's *Black Iris*, Iraq's *Baghdad Burning*, and Tunisia's *Tunisian Girl*, to name just a few, played a prominent role in shaping local and foreign perceptions of their countries' politics and society. These bloggers provided articulate and valuable accounts of "life on the ground" that propelled a number of them into celebrity status as activists both within their own countries and in the international media. Although many of these bloggers did not always represent wider Arab public opinion, their influence on public debate was pervasive.[25] In the lead-up to the Arab uprisings, many blogs highlighted the mass frustration that was brewing just below the surface. Often critical of governments' economic policies, these blogs were among the most insightful views of how Arabs perceived their governments. Not surprisingly, many of the bloggers were university-educated youth; according to one study, over 90 per cent of Arab bloggers had an undergraduate university degree and more than a third had a graduate degree.[26]

Blogs are now part of a larger technological ecosystem that is changing the landscape of Arab media and public discourse on key issues. It is not uncommon to find blogs that incorporate or respond to viral cell phone videos, Facebook campaigns, YouTube videos, and Tweets that, in turn, generate and reinforce public debate that runs parallel to traditional media reporting. This networked public sphere moves at a pace that Arab leaders and censors cannot keep up with, and contains content on which mainstream media has little input.[27] To get a sense of the popularity and influence of these blogs, 25 per cent of respondents to an Arab-wide poll conducted by the Dubai School of Government in 2013, said they visited educational blogs and magazines daily, 24 per cent said they did so at least several times a week, and 17 per cent did several times a day.[28]

During the Egyptian revolution of January 2011, numerous online campaigns motivated people to go to Tahrir Square and call for the overthrow of the Mubarak regime. Notably, an online Facebook campaign, "We are all Khaled Said," was dedicated to the memory of a young man who witnessed an illegal transaction among Alexandria police in mid-2010, and was then taken out of an Internet café, brutally beaten, and eventually killed by the police. Said's family posted a cell phone photo of his mutilated corpse online, and the picture went viral both by text messaging and through Facebook. The Facebook page dedicated to Said's memory was created by Wael Ghonim, a young Google executive living in the UAE, and the page soon became a campaign for human rights and government accountability in Egypt. It garnered hundreds of thousands of followers before the outbreak of the revolution, but the image and memory of Khaled Said would resonate further after the Tunisian revolution, when Said's story was paralleled by the fate of Mohamed Bouazizi.

Although many attribute the online campaign to memorialize Said as a key factor in the Egyptian revolution, it was the impassioned words of a twenty-six-year-old woman that truly sparked the sentiment of a nation. Her name was Asmaa Mahfouz, and she struck a chord with millions of Egyptians when she uploaded a video on YouTube days before Egyptians from all walks of life marched to Tahrir Square to demand Mubarak's resignation. Mahfouz was a member of the April 6th movement, youth activists who have been running political campaigns online to fight for workers' rights in the Egyptian industrial town of Mahalla al-Kubra since 2008. The movement was instrumental to the Egyptian uprising as it called for and organized the flash mob demonstrations and coordinated Facebook campaigns that helped get people to demonstrate against the regime. As a young woman who appealed to men and women to demonstrate their self-dignity, pride, and intellect, Mahfouz spoke to the heart of what many Arab people had felt for decades. Mahfouz was not your typical political organizer. She infused political activism with nationalism and, more important, with notions of honour. She reminded millions of how the regime had slowly chipped away at their sense of being, of how it had reduced people to a nadir in a sea of powerlessness. Her appeal resonated with Egyptians, reminding them that there is strength in numbers as well as in a commitment to pride and dignity. She also reminded them that, as individuals, they could become the next victims of state security, that no one was immune to the abuse of police power – and this became a focal point of the mobilization and mass demonstrations.

Mahfouz's video blog was unlike others because she spoke to both the Egyptian people and to the regime. Without the power of the online platform to post and share these political pieces, there would have been no way for views like Mahfouz's to enter the public space. Moreover, she quickly became but one of many voices in this changing public landscape: in 2014, for example, during a political campaign, Saudi nationals – boldly raising their national identification cards as a sign that they were not afraid of government reprisals – posted YouTube videos of themselves criticizing state corruption, nepotism, low wages, and high unemployment. These videos went viral, attracting attention from all over the world. For example, a video by Abdulaziz Mohammed Al Dosari, which has been viewed 1.8 million times, directly addressed the monarch in broken but emphatic English: "Until when we will have to beg you to give us from this petroleum … Brother, give us some of the oil wealth you and your sons play with."

Many other Saudi men and women have posted similar videos in which they openly criticize government policies.[29] Often, online campaigns are calls for freedom and a fundamentally different way of governing. One of the boldest was a Twitter campaign begun in early 2013 by Waleed Abu Alkhair – with the hashtag "the salary is not enough" (in Arabic) – that generated more than seventeen million responses in just a few months. In fact, Saudi Arabia, with 1.9 million accounts, has the highest percentage of Twitter users in the Arab region. Despite Alkhair's arrest, responses keep coming, making it impossible to arrest all of the campaign's online proponents or "retweeters."

Another Saudi Twitter activist, Loujain (@LoujainHathloul), also used social media to challenge discrimination against women. Through Twitter, Instagram, Keek videos, and Facebook, she challenged the Saudi government to recognize women as individuals with rights, not as dependants of male partners and/or guardians. In my interview with this bright and passionate young woman, she told me what motivated her:

> We Saudi women were so use[d] to hiding behind avatars and pseudonyms like "Brave Woman" to express our views on social media that I realized that this further perpetuated the government's policies about women. Women in Saudi have no identity, no voice, no face, and by using avatars and pseudonyms we were also denying our existence as persons. So I decided to call out my Saudi sisters, and said, "hey, at least use your name." I wanted to push people, especially women, to not hide. So I took videos and pictures of myself without a *hijab*, used my real first and last name, and discussed topics like the absurdity of needing a male guardian to authorize my travel, accept education grants, or even to take a job.

Loujain not only challenged the Saudi government; she also stirred public discussion about women's freedoms in the Kingdom. With millions of hits, retweets, and quotes, Loujain successfully started a movement that encourages women to use their real names throughout social media. By confronting her country's policies and social norms about perpetuating female anonymity, Loujain influenced many people to view women as persons.

Freedom from What? For What?

When young Arabs took to the streets and to the web demanding *hurriya* (freedom), what exactly did they mean?

Before the Arab Spring it was common to hear Arab youth say, in defiance of their elders, "*Ana hurr*," which translates to "I'm free." Yet, the reality is that many Arab youth yearned to escape from the economic, political, and social shackles that stunted their access to a better life. Most Arab countries were deemed "not free" by the independent watchdog organization Freedom House. Morocco, Tunisia, Libya, Lebanon, and Kuwait were regarded as "partly free," while the rest of the Arab region scored poorly on indices related to fostering civil liberty, transparency, press freedom, and civil society organizations.

A persistent and common political and economic concern of many Arabs, young and old alike, is the lack of government accountability. In a 2011 survey of 1,445 middle-class adults in Egypt, Saudi Arabia, and Morocco, 73 per cent of the respondents believed that their government was corrupt, and an almost equal percentage felt it was non-transparent and published inaccurate information.[30] Indeed, on all questions of the survey that inquired into people's faith in government institutions and processes, the responses were overwhelmingly negative.[31] When asked about their faith in public officials to "support those who want to succeed in life," 60 per cent held negative views about official policies. A similar response was given to the question of whether opportunities are available to "those who seek success."[32] This deteriorating faith in government capability and widespread belief in government corruption as a key impediment to positive economic and social reform is particularly prevalent among Arab youth. Many perceive that state corruption has stunted their opportunity to succeed, and they long for a political and economic system that levels the playing field.

Not all Arab governments are entirely corrupt, and not all are corrupt in the same way. A common definition of corruption, as articulated by the highly reputed Transparency International Index, is "abuse of entrusted power for private gain." By this measure some Arab countries – including Sudan, Yemen, Libya, Egypt, and Syria – are among the worst in the world, and it is no coincidence that calls for the overthrow of the regime were strongest in most of these countries. Other Arab countries fare better on the corruption index and actually rank above the world average – for example, rates of corruption in the Gulf states are comparable to those in eastern and southern Europe.

Different types of corruption also prevail in different Arab countries. Grand corruption, where elite groups and preferred families get inside land deals or lucrative licences or business contracts, was common in Tunisia, Egypt, and Libya, where governments were overthrown. For example, before his ouster, Tunisian president Zine el-Abidine Ben Ali and the family of his wife, Leila Trabelsi, controlled a number of companies that used their government allies to legislate fixed prices, thus preventing competition. This allowed the ruling family to earn 21 per cent of domestic net profits, although these companies contributed only 3 per cent of the national output.[33] In Egypt some of the anger was directed at the Mubarak family and its inner circle for profiting from exclusive licences to import and export certain goods and services. Many Egyptian entrepreneurs, small and medium-sized enterprises, and rising businesses complained of a glass ceiling that allowed elite cronies to block their success unless they provided kickbacks to powerful stakeholders, including Mubarak's sons.

Paying bribes at a public office to get paperwork processed was all too prevalent in pre-revolutionary Egypt, Libya, and Syria. Often, petty corruption was sugar-coated, dismissed as tips or gratuities. I myself once had such an experience going through the terminal at Cairo airport. A police officer who was "helping" me move my bags through the security area asked for something "sweet" for his hard work. If I did not comply, he informed me, "the paperwork might take too long to process." Travelling through Syria, we often gave lemons or cigarettes to officers who stopped our vehicle for "routine screening." Such gifts are common in certain parts of the Middle East, and those who do not offer them often face long delays in getting where they want to go. Of course, such petty corruption does not prevail everywhere. In the Gulf, for example, where most public sector workers are nationals and paid relatively well, "tips" are not well received. Unaware of Jordanian mores, an acquaintance of mine tried to pass 20 dinars to a police officer to help get us out of a minor traffic violation. The offer was taken as a great insult in a sector dominated by local tribes that take pride in their profession.

Dealing with the subtleties of petty corruption has become a daily routine for many Arab citizens. For youth, who have little pocket money but a growing sense of individuality and pride in their level of education, these kinds of interactions with officials feel especially intrusive and demeaning, and many took to blogging and documenting such abuses of power online. The irony of government employees in positions of relative power probing for petty bribes is not lost on a generation of savvy young people. Although I doubt previous generations of Arabs internalized these customs as morally right, there remains among the older generation a sense of resignation and acceptance that does not persist among today's youth.

Not only do Arab youth chafe at petty official corruption and the lack of government accountability, they also face unemployment rates that are higher than those of any other demographic group in the world and much higher than faced by their elders, who were often offered guaranteed public sector employment. Needless to say, the job market is extremely competitive, but even tougher for those who are poor, live in rural areas, or do not come from families with strong connections to elite circles. Meritocracy simply does not prevail in most of the Arab world, where networks of patronage determine who gets scarce or decent employment. Searching for work is a demoralizing experience for many young graduates. As Emad from Jordan told me, "I graduated in the top of my class, but I see others get the better jobs because their father knows someone, has a *wasta* [a powerful network] or because they have money." I often heard this sort of sentiment – the perception that others get ahead based not on merit, but on favouritism, clientelism, and nepotism – in my conversations with young people. In Egypt, Sohair, a twenty-four-year-old business student graduate, casually noted that she could not get a job as a teaching assistant in her university because there were not enough positions after all of the professors' children were appointed. This resort to nepotism eats at the core of societal progress and success – namely, ambition. In Morocco, Mourad, an unemployed thirty-something without a university degree, said: "Go to Parliament and you will see demonstrators. They are the ones with undergraduate degrees and with no jobs." To this, an eighteen-year-old, religiously devout high school student named Hatem added: "While the minister inside doesn't even have a bachelor's degree."

Getting a job in the Gulf, where labour shortages persist, is somewhat easier for youth, but decent or desirable employment often depends on whom your father knows, what tribe you come from, or your parents' professional network. In some countries, being born into an unfavourable sectarian community or religious minority can also limit one's career options or chances of success. As a Bahraini activist exiled in Washington, DC, said to me: "It was insulting that, as a Shia, I was not welcomed into the security sector or military, while the authorities hired Pakistanis and Jordanians to 'defend' my country, from 'my people'."

Thus, behind many of the cries of freedom of the Arab youth who took to the streets and cyberspace was the desire to be free from government corruption, to compete based on merit, and to alter the social contract. When the Arab Spring was at its zenith, many Western policy-makers suggested that the Arab world wanted democracy, and, indeed, there is plenty of survey evidence to suggest that Arabs, particularly youth, see the merits of a democratic system in remedying the failures of institutions and the challenges posed by patronage and corruption. Leading analysts and pundits in Washington also gave the US government credit for funding the promotion of democracy in certain countries in the decade preceding the Arab Spring. Yet, democracy was not on most Arabs' list of demands, and despite the uprisings US foreign policy was in favour of "democratic evolution, not revolution."[34] Moreover, democracy promotion programs were insufficient to trigger the mass frustration and mobilization required to demand regime change. Also, the academic literature on democratization in the Arab region perpetuates confusion about what triggers to look for, the very applicability of the concept of democracy in the Western liberal sense to the Arab region, and the tools and methods appropriate to assess such a loaded and normative term as "democracy" in a region where there are real empirical lags.[35]

Irrespective of Western policy initiatives and academic debates, it is not the case that Arabs do not want to live in a democracy. Quite the contrary: in Pew Research Center surveys conducted annually since 2010, an overwhelming proportion of Arab respondents agree that "democracy is preferable to any other kind of government." Moreover, support for democracy is highest among Arab youth: at the height of the optimism surrounding the Arab Spring, surveys showed that 92 per cent of Arab youth wanted democracy and felt it was the most important change they would like to see in their countries.[36] Indeed, when asked in 2010 what they believed was "the biggest obstacle facing the Middle East," Arab youth cited "lack of democracy" as the second-most-critical issue, after "civil unrest" and well before either "lack of Arab unity" or the "Israeli-Palestinian conflict."[37] There were no discernible differences between the answers of Arab youth in the oil-rich Gulf region and those elsewhere, which suggests it is a myth that Arabs in oil-rich countries are more apathetic about democracy than are their brethren in poorer countries. Indeed, on almost all questions about politics, the survey revealed only very small differences in viewpoints among Arab youth, regardless of their country or income levels.

So, Arabs desire democracy. But do they desire it enough to create the political organizations and collective action needed to build the foundation of democracy? In time, yes, and I believe it will come when the Arab youth of today are at the helm. Granted, youth activism, civil society organizations, broad-based political parties that appeal to national integration, not particularistic identities, and key institutional structures to support democracy (such as an independent judiciary) are all in their nascent stage in the Arab region. Nevertheless, they are on the rise, complemented most importantly by changes in culture and values about how things ought to be. As I show in Chapter 4, new cultural values, among other key factors, are shaping the identity of Arab youth in progressive ways that are propelling political change from the bottom up. As Kristin Diwan has aptly put it, "[t]he new youth culture values self-direction over control, networks over hierarchy, and transparency over secrecy."[38]

There is a great deal of work to be done if the Arab world's demographic dividend and cultural shift in values and attitudes are to manifest themselves in positive democratic reforms. Academics and pundits alike have looked for the spark – perhaps struck by professional associations, non-governmental organizations, and civil society actors as possible precursors of game-changing political parties – that might set off such a democratic wave, but so far have noted, more than anything, the challenges such groups face in confronting entrenched state power. However, key institutional and structural foundations of democracy are also dependent on ideas percolating from the bottom up, especially from Arab youth. Here is where we find signs of progressive change.

It is the Arab region's demographic dividend that will push for real, sustained change. After all, for a parliament to function properly, the give-and-take of ideas needs to be forged; for broad-based political parties to rise, individuals need to see themselves as citizens; for human rights to take root, people need to respect the place of minorities and women; for the rule of law to be respected, people need to believe in the universality, meritocracy, and transparency of the legal system; for a free press to thrive, individuals need to appreciate the critical role of journalism and the media as a political check on abuses of power, not just as a means to undermine the security of the state. Is the Arab world there yet? Absolutely not. Are Arab youth willing to demand all of the above, with or without the backing of organized groups? Absolutely.

Conclusion

How calls for the free exchange of ideas and information will lead to real, sustained democratic change in the Arab world is still a work in progress. As Brookings Institution Fellow Stephen Grand aptly puts it, "It is far easier to mobilize citizens to unseat a despotic regime than to construct a liberal democratic order in its place – one is an act of destruction, the other an act of construction."[39] Arab youth have yet to enter the phase of construction, but they are poised to push past the threshold for change in their communities and beyond. As the next chapter illuminates, Arab youth value and perceive the world in fundamentally new ways that offer good reasons for hope and optimism for social, political, and economic reform throughout the Middle East.

Arab youth are creating political communities and networks of information that are similar to the political organization of parties and unions seen a century ago in the West. What started with bloggers and Internet forums has developed into a larger ecosystem of online activists without a political banner, but who share one overriding concern: the political future of the Arab region and the changes that need to take place. Technology has provided the tools to communicate within and across these communities, and has amplified the call for change from the bottom up. Although our impulse is to pigeonhole groups as liberals, leftists, conservatives, Islamists, and so on, to do so is to overlook the wider movement of youth who do find these labels neither comforting nor applicable.

Arab youth want change. Undoubtedly, they need to articulate how the future of the Arab region ought to look. The preconditions for democracy are still very much in their infancy in the Arab world, but it would be wrong to assume, as many Western analysts and political scientists do, that, because we cannot place them in ideal, Western types of political groupings, Arab youth will turn to complacency or disorder. Arab youth are more politically engaged than their elders ever were. Instead of traditional Western forms of political organization, they are using new tools, including digital technology, to further the conversation about the need for political reform. Young Arabs are weary of political strongmen and a political discourse that demands that they give up their freedoms for the sake of state security. Instead, they are challenging their governments, making their own demands for the elimination of corruption, nepotism, and non-accountability, which they see as the real impediments to economic and political progress.

chapter four

Identity

As economic liberalization and the flow of ideas about freedom sweep through the Arab world, Arab youth often find others' views about their identity trapped within a circular conversation about modernity and tradition. It is a conversation that has less and less purchase on how youth live their day-to-day lives, which some religious leaders, politicians, and elders have labelled as moving towards "Western," "un-Arab," or "un-Islamic" values. Yet, Western perceptions about the Arab world as fundamentalist, rigid, and backward also fail to describe the identity and lives of young Arabs today. Samuel Huntington's "clash of civilizations" thesis, which claimed that conflict between Western values and those of Islam was a foregone conclusion, remains too easily accepted in parts of the West, despite its problematic premise and prediction. For most Arab youth, Huntington's thesis is antithetical to their reality. Many young Arabs find it perfectly compatible to identify as a person of faith who also holds modern and progressive values (such as wanting democracy), has a cosmopolitan identity, and respects individual liberties. Similarly, Arab youth are capable of synthesizing a deep commitment to their families and communities and the pursuit of individual freedoms. They see no contradiction in the mixing of identities such as modern, Western, family-oriented, religious, and Arab.

Yes, there are those in the Arab region who want to adopt a rigid interpretation of Islam – often lumped into a category called "Salafists" – who want to turn back the clock of globalization and reject

Western liberal values and beliefs. We must remember, however, that similar types of communities exist in the West – Amish, Old Order Mennonite, and the like – who believe that their views about dress, technology, family relations, and so on keep them closer to God. These groups do not represent the views of the mainstream, but still have a right to practise their faith so long as it does not impede the rights of others, does not require others to practise or follow the same rules, and, of course, is non-violent.

The views of Arab youth about religion and society and their aspirations for the future are often more progressive than Western analysts give them credit for, despite the presence of rigid views of Islam practised by a small minority, like Salafists, who, for example, promote segregation of the sexes. For many youth who have a strong sense of faith in Islam, it is an attraction to principles of social justice that strengthens their identity as Muslims. With so much corruption and inequity surrounding them, religion provides a useful moral compass to redirect their energies and faith in society. For Arab youth who are disappointed by their leaders, their religious identity becomes a source of pride and hope for a just and dignified society. This does not mean Arab youth are willing to be preached at from the pulpit. They want to discuss and debate Islam and its merits to find its utility and, at times, its indifference to modern challenges. It is not uncommon to hear Arab youth today debate their older family members, whereas previous generations dared not question elders as a sign of respect. They tell their parents: "I know your view, but convince me why this is better for me in the long run." They are also more apt to question governments and clergy, rather than pay deference to authorities for the sake of stability, calm, and order. Indeed, the erosion of deference in the region is increasingly palpable. To youth, this is not a sign of disrespect, but of their growing intelligence and awareness of the world, their questioning of social and normative givens, and their quest for knowledge and answers to religious and moral ambiguities. Most Arab governments, parents, and clergy have yet to view this development as a sign of youth's intelligence and awareness; instead, they see it as a form of subversion, a move to undermine the authority or sanctity of the state.

In this chapter, I want to highlight the ways in which Arab youth view their identity in holistic terms and their increasing tendency to reject binary and reductive labels such as Eastern versus Western, civilized versus traditional, and religion versus reason. For Arab youth, Benjamin Barber's *Jihad vs. McWorld* or Thomas Freidman's *Lexus and the Olive Tree* fail to acknowledge the nuances of their society. For all of the modernizing forces brought on by globalization, Arab youth are often passionate about securing dignity while pursuing social justice. Dignity, to them, is respect for and recognition of their rights as individuals, while social justice is the pursuit of equity and fairness in a society free from corruption and nepotism. To achieve both, they do not feel it necessary or desirable to sacrifice values such as family, honour, and tradition that are so important to Arabs. But they do seek equal opportunity to compete without issues of class, gender, ethnicity, or sect impeding their pursuit. This fundamental right was one of the motivating factors behind the Arab Spring, and it will continue to motivate youth regardless of the domestic and regional challenges they face.

"Secular" Arab Society

Compared to decades past, the early twenty-first century has seen a noticeable resurgence of public displays of religious faith in the Arab region. In Cairo, Tunis, or Baghdad in the 1970s and 1980s, it was rare to see a young woman wearing a *hijab*, let alone a *niqab*. Outside the Gulf states – Kuwait, the United Arab Emirates, Saudi Arabia, Oman, Qatar, and Bahrain – most Arab countries practised and enforced secularism on their citizens. Women and men were encouraged to set aside religious identities in favour of state identities, which cultivated the idea of citizenship in many Arab countries and helped Arab governments subdue an important potential political opponent: the religious clergy and their followers. The Gulf countries, in contrast, used religion selectively and strategically to bolster their legitimacy by co-opting religious authorities and movements. The picture of the Arab region – outside the Gulf – was therefore of a secularist society. This was more illusion than reality, and tainted with discrimination towards devotees of Islam and with a select view of urban, upper-class Arab society.

In the 1970s and 1980s, however, only a minority of Arabs lived in urban areas. The rural majority was relatively unaffected by many of the secularizing trends that pervaded Marrakesh, Cairo, Damascus, and Baghdad. In rural areas, most still practised their religion, and many women chose to wear a *hijab*. At the time, Arab governments did not view these rural populations as a political threat, and they were usually permitted to follow their religious and other traditions on their own terms. In most urban areas outside the Gulf, Muslim women who chose to wear a headscarf and Muslim men who chose to grow a beard were seen as those who defied secularism, and were targets of discrimination by secular governments. One never saw a woman wearing a *hijab* in government-controlled television dramas or films, except in the role of a housemaid or elderly woman, a practice that still continues in less rigid ways in current Arab programs and movies.

Similarly, news broadcasters on state television channels never wore a headscarf or long beard. Women and men in positions of authority, including ministers, university deans, and heads of state-owned enterprises, were forbidden, either by law or by custom, to display their religious faith outwardly – a situation that remained the case for Egyptian broadcasters until the overthrow of Mubarak in 2011. To succeed, one needed to suppress one's faith or be a closeted Muslim – a belief that continues to prevail in many parts of the region outside the Gulf, particularly among the older generation. This is not to deny that many religious minorities, such as Christians and Jews, as well as atheists and agnostics, were also discriminated against by the state and/or society. But it is important to understand that Islam – the faith of the majority of Arabs – was viewed as a political and social threat in most of the Arab region, and that religious practice remains an important context in contemporary debates about identity and the pursuit of dignity and social justice.

One memorable example of this tension between religious expression and societal pressure was the decision in the early 2000s by prominent Al-Jazeera news anchor Khadija Ben Ghanna to wear a *hijab* after years of success as an uncovered woman. This would have been unheard of on a state television station, but her defiance of secularism on a private satellite station still caused a stir. It is a matter of great irony that, in a region where the majority of women wear and support the *hijab*, the choice of a news anchor to wear one on television could cause such worry and fear among secular governments and certain members of the public.[1]

Political pressure to maintain the illusion of secularism and contain the reality of the increased religiosity of Arab society served to increase the alienation of people from their governments. State pressure by some governments to suppress or "tame" people of faith created a great deal of social anomie and frustration. Moreover, many Arab Muslims felt that religiosity, the pursuit of which they believed was dignified and respectful, was slowly but surely being turned into a political threat by their governments and socio-economic elites. For many Arabs, the call for justice and social dignity was also a call for governments to better reflect their societies, to be more responsive to people's identities, and to narrow the widening gap between the elites and the masses, which included, in no small part, calls for governments to view the religious as citizens with the right to practise their faith, rather than as potential threats to order. The tension between state-sanctioned views of ideals of Arab life and the way people actually lived and identified with their society further perpetuated perceptions among the public that Arab governments did not, or simply refused to, understand their people.

Some might argue that a secular society is a progressive, modern one, but it seems unlikely that banning citizens from expressing their faith can hold up as a progressive value. Nevertheless, discrimination against people of faith in the Arab region was – and remains, albeit to a lesser extent than in the past – most visible at the higher levels of the social strata and among the older generation. Discrimination against religious expression was further reinforced in state-sanctioned images and stereotypes found on television, on billboards showcasing the typical Arab family, and even through the presentation of the wives and families of Arab leaders. As a well-to-do fifty-year-old female friend in Cairo recently said to me, "It seemed like the higher one wanted to move up the social ladder and to be a part of the elite community in exclusive social clubs and posh social circles, one had to flagrantly defy Islamic tenants by wearing shorter and shorter skirts." People of faith were portrayed, and often viewed by the urban elite, as "backward," "uncivilized," or "unmodern," and the social pressure to conform to the dominant trend of wearing Western attire and denying one's religious heritage was the only way to progress up the social, political, and economic ladder – though, again, I am talking about countries outside the Gulf region. Discrimination against people of faith was felt in all levels of society.

I recall visiting the University of Jordan for a semester in the early 1990s, where I met women who chose to wear a *hijab*. Some of them commuted from the countryside, and wore a headscarf to protect against unwarranted advances by men on public transport. They did not always feel a religious or spiritual affinity for the *hijab*, but wore it to be more "liberated" as they moved throughout this socially conservative country. Public transportation in many Arab countries is an undignified experience for women, who often experience harassment, if not outright assault. For some, wearing the headscarf helps prevent such incidents. Of course, women should not feel the need to cover their bodies or hair in order to prevent harassment by men; the fault here lies with the men who do the harassing, as well as with a patriarchal and misogynistic system that produces and perpetuates such behaviour. The fact remains, however, that, for many Arab women, wearing a *hijab* gives them greater mobility in public places. In contrast, women from elite circles who use private transport or socialize in private circles do not need the *hijab* to grant them their mobility.

Of course, some women choose to wear a *hijab* out of a sense of spirituality and devotion to God. These more devout women are growing in number, adding to the religious revivalism taking place in the Arab region. A young woman named Eman, from an upper-middle-class merchant family, became a dear friend when I visited the University of Jordan in the early 1990s. At the time, Eman complained to me that professors in the commerce department ignored women who wore a headscarf, and confided that one of her professors had told her: "Why do you study commerce? Why not go study Islamic *sharia*? There's no place for a woman to study commerce and practise business if wearing a headscarf." The discrimination was worse for women who chose to cover their face by wearing a *niqab*, particularly in universities outside the Gulf. In some cases, as at the American University of Cairo (AUC), the *niqab* was forbidden, and a woman who wore one was denied entry. An outright ban on the *niqab* was also in place in Tunisian universities. Eman continued her education in the commerce department, but confided that too often it crossed her mind to remove her headscarf in order to secure better job opportunities. She once told me, "If I immigrated to Canada, I'd have an easier time wearing my *hijab* there than I would in this Muslim-majority country. You have human rights in Canada that we do not yet have."

Things have changed quite drastically since that time. In Egypt, 94.6 per cent of young Muslim women now wear a *hijab*, while 5.1 per cent wear a *niqab* and only 0.4 per cent wear no head covering. When asked why they wore a *hijab*, the overwhelming response was either "personal choice," listening to sermons, or reading religious books. Only 10 per cent stated that "parents either pushed or persuaded them" to do so, and this pressure was highest in rural and underdeveloped areas.[2] During my travels, I met a twenty-two-year-old woman named Hania, who studied architecture at the AUC. In her teenage years, Hania attended, often held at another woman's home, informal religious discussions of the Quran. At these purely voluntary meetings, women could discuss Islam in an open, non-intimidating environment. The point here is not to emphasize the interpretive and religious content of these informal classes, but the style of their delivery. Islam was discussed, more than taught, and the conversations were very different from the types of sermons men heard in the local mosques. Hence, while most of these women-led meetings emphasized the spiritual side of Islam, with a focus on love and devotion, sermons in the mosques were led by a religious leader, an *imam*, who would yell passionately about religion and focus on draconian laws of dos and don'ts or the political aspects of Islamic teachings.

Women-led religious classes have become very influential in the Arab region, and are a key driver of the revival of Islam today. In a survey of young Egyptian men and women, it was found that women were more likely (by fourteen percentage points) than their male counterparts to pray.[3] Bypassing state controls, this more spiritual view of Islam that many women have adopted has also found its way into private satellite television and programming. Channels such as *Iqraa*, *Al-Majd*, *Al-Risala*, and *4Shabab* provide twenty-four-hour programming about Islam and, unlike previous religious programming by Saudi or Gulf state channels, offer discussion and debate about the challenges of applying religion in everyday life. These programs tend to be more conversational or motivational, more tolerant than absolute, and more spiritual than political. The stars of these satellite channels are mild-talking preachers, and include a higher number of young men and women. These programs also appeal more to youth and women than they do to older men through their combination of interactive formats with audience members, including on-screen, sometimes spontaneous, prayers with hands open (*dua'a*). Compare this to the much more rigid programming in Saudi Arabia and the Gulf states that features a live feed of prayers performed by men in the more institutionalized setting of a mosque.[4] Arab youth are increasingly critical about such religious messages and the way in which they are delivered. Again, as deference erodes among Arab youth, more informal, spiritual approaches to Islamic teachings are cultivating a new kind of Islam, one with which Arab youth increasingly identify. These types of Islamic programs are more progressive than their institutionalized counterparts, and signal the direction in which discourse about religion and identity is heading.

To take one example of the new breed of broadcasters, Mustafa Hosny is a young preacher whose program appears on satellite TV stations as well as online. The program quite consciously borrows a modern aesthetic, using clips of everyday life in the Middle East set to upbeat music. Wearing trendy clothing and a trimmed beard, Hosny speaks softly and eloquently. The show starts with viewers' letters and questions, and uses real life situations to explain the spiritual meaning of Islamic tenets. Unlike the classical Arabic used by preachers on state television, Hosny's use of colloquial Arabic is accessible to people, especially those youth who are losing touch with classical, formal Arabic. In a number of episodes, Hosny presents his show on a boat featuring panoramic views while he speaks about Islamic teachings and philosophies. Figures like Hosny are creating a new market for spiritual teachings outside the sanctioned messaging of governments generally found in mosques, and indeed many of the older state-sanctioned preachers are losing their impact among the young.

Yet many Arabs raised in the secularist tradition that prevailed in the mid-twentieth century view religious revivalism as an ominous sign. Sitting with a well-to-do Cairo family, I heard several hesitant remarks from older members about how Islamicization had changed their city. As one sixty-something woman said to me, "you know, we all wore miniskirts in our twenties, and now my granddaughter thinks the *hijab* is fashionable. Something isn't right!" In speaking critically about this shift, people often blame Saudi Arabia for "exporting" these types of religious views through financial contributions to mosques, media outlets, and so on. Others blame the returning tide of workers who, after a few years in the Gulf states, return home with more conservative views.

I do not mean to discount these as potential factors in the religious revival, but the role of private religious instruction and discussion (primarily by women) and the youth-focused programs seen on satellite television remain forgotten and undertheorized phenomena that help to illuminate the resurgence of Islamic identities in the Arab world. Moreover, this resurgence has been nonviolent, transcending nationalist and/or contractarian politics – whereby citizens trade rights for the security and protection of government – in favour of political attitudes based more on social justice, and can be seen as an evolution arising from increased societal debate and rising levels of female education, particularly in urban settings. This helps explain, for example, why a 2009 study of Arab bloggers conducted by Harvard University found a high number of supporters of the Muslim Brotherhood were, in fact, young women. Moreover, the same study found that many of the female bloggers chose to write about their devotion to Islam and to explain their piousness.[5] One should not mistake these blogs as antifeminist; on the contrary, these are women who celebrate their religiosity in an empowered way, who want to lead their communities, and who demand gender equality.

Where state media has suppressed information and knowledge about faith, evangelical preachers on satellite television are feeding a hunger for spirituality outside the mosque. In addition, as the discourse surrounding human rights has grown around the globe, so has the idea that people have a right to practise their faith. Nonetheless, while the discourse about faith pervades Arab society, the underlying social prejudice against people of faith, particularly the higher one goes up the socio-economic ladder and among the older generation, remains.

In her second year of studies at the AUC, Hania went against the common trend and opted to remove her *hijab* after wearing it for six years. I asked her why. She said: "People only saw me as a girl who wears a *hijab* and couldn't see me as an individual. People assumed that I wasn't fun, sporty, or creative. I didn't like the way people assumed things about my personality." Hania admitted that peer pressure at the AUC, where the children of elite, typically more liberal families tend to go, might have shaped her views. Unable to join in many of the types of activities her classmates attended, she felt that wearing a *hijab* inhibited movement in her social circle. Moreover, according to Hania, "Had I attended Cairo University or another public university, I would have felt the reverse kind of pressure to not remove my headscarf." This was a sentiment repeated by Dana, a twenty-one-year-old student at Yarmouk University, a public university located in Irbid, Jordan's second-largest city. There, wearing a *hijab* is the norm. Dana lamented that the private German university in Jordan her brother attended has a more relaxed environment in which girls do not wear a *hijab* and the two sexes intermingle. Discrimination against women who wear a *hijab* is still evident throughout the non-Gulf Arab region, but it is in decline as more and more women openly practise their Islamic faith. The important point here is that many youth do not have the same inhibitions against the *hijab* that their parents or grandparents had, particularly those raised in cities. Today's youth see this as a spiritual choice, and reject the idea that one should be forced to wear it or not wear it.

It cannot be emphasized enough that non-Muslims and Muslims from smaller sects – such as Shiites, Alawites, and Druze – face more discrimination in the Arab region than they used to. Rightly or wrongly, the tide of Islamic revivalism is often blamed for this increased hostility to religious minorities.[6] It is also worth pointing out, however, that such discrimination is most acutely felt in areas where civil wars, revolutions, or violent upheavals have taken place. In Lebanon, Iraq, and Syria, for example, historical and academic analyses concur that the source of conflict was never a religious one, but religious communities are pitted against each other in conflicts over geopolitics and dwindling resources, and reflecting a more general breakdown in law and order. Sadly, there is now a higher migration, both forced and voluntary, of Arab Christians, Copts, Jews, and smaller religious sects, who are leaving the region at an unprecedented pace. Many lament that the identity of Arabs as a diverse mosaic is in decline and that the discrimination felt by religious minorities, atheists, and agnostics is on the rise.

Finding the right balance in respecting people's faith is something that the Arab region is grappling with, and the discourse surrounding this challenge is quite similar to the one we see developing in Western multicultural societies. Most such societies, however, are liberal democracies that generally safeguard freedom of expression and provide minorities legal protection against discrimination. Too often, as well, the rise of Islamic spirituality is confused with the rise of militant Islam on the part of radicalized groups in war zones, separatist forces, or in places of government neglect, such as are found in Libya, Egypt's Sinai Peninsula, eastern Syria, western Iraq, and Yemen. For outside observers, nuance is key to understanding the differences between the more prevalent peaceful and spiritual religious revivalism and the smaller, violent, and radicalized movements that have sprung up throughout the region. Western media misperceptions are not solely to blame for confusing spiritual revivalism with the growth of militant violence – many Arab governments also conveniently use the rise of Islam, writ large, to suggest the presence of an ominous political and strategic threat.[7] I discuss the geopolitical considerations of religious revivalism in the Arab world in the final chapter; here, I want to point out that spiritual interpretations of Islam provide key philosophical tenets for increasing calls for dignity and social justice. Furthermore, decades of political discourse and visual misrepresentation of observant Muslims have also contributed to the social and political alienation of the Arab masses from their governments and leaders.

Unlike previous generations, today's Arab youth do not have the same conceptions about the separation of religion, faith, and secularism. Granted, there remains strong, state-sanctioned messaging that religiosity brings social and political ills. Nevertheless, my sense is that Arab youth tend to be more inclined to reject this type of binary messaging and to accept the religiosity of others. Their demographic growth could bring new values and attitudes about faith to public discourse. And with their increased travel and mobility, many Arab youth are seeing the inherent value in a pluralistic society, in multicultural values practised in Western countries, and in the protection of minority rights. It is the more moderate and inclusive views espoused by so many Arab youth that keeps me optimistic about the future of the region.

Mecca Mall

Many Arab youth have an uncanny way of mixing both Eastern and Western identities in their lives. They often seamlessly traverse both worlds, and do so in their day-to-day lives. For example, although many young Arab women choose to wear a *hijab*, they are likely to do so in conjunction with fashionable trends found in Western-style retail stores. I asked a perceptive friend in Amman what was going on with young Arab women today. I was surprised to learn that many young women throughout the region, from Rabat to Cairo to Amman to Dubai, were wearing a *hijab* with tight blue jeans and trendy tops – cues taken from stylish Western magazines. According to my friend, young Arab women today are "Mecca above the neck, and Mecca Mall below the neck" – certainly not the image I had of the conservative wearers of the *hijab*. Mecca Mall is a trendy shopping place in Amman that houses branches of Western retail stores. The visibility of such stores increasingly erodes the contradiction between wearing a *hijab* as well as trendy clothes from popular Western outlets such as Zara, H & M, Mango, and DKNY, which launched an Islamic Ramadan collection for the summer and fall 2014. Geared towards urban women, the collection includes colourful trench coats paired with trousers, khakis, and stylish *hijabs*.

This apparent incongruity is becoming more and more normal in the Arab world, and is emblematic of the balance between Eastern and Western identities that young people increasingly exhibit and advertising specialists agree are shaping their purchasing behaviour. Market researchers looking at consumers in five Arab countries have found that Arabs are unique, global consumers who share values such as an emphasis on the importance of family, an attachment to traditions that are adaptive to modernity, a high regard for education, a desire for spaces for self-expression, and an attraction to Western products.[8] Beyond these commonalities, the researchers segmented Arabs into four broad consumer types: religious conservatives, primarily older men, who are "anti-media and information-averse"; societal conformists, mostly men from lower socio-economic groups, particularly in rural areas; New Age Muslims, who are upper or middle class, urbanite, and mainly female, who like modern trends and are religious; and liberals, who are urban, young, and affluent.[9] As Table 4.1 indicates, not all five countries in the survey have the same mix of consumer types. Religious conservatives are primarily of an older demographic group and will have less purchasing power over time, whereas demographic trends predict that both New Age Muslims and liberals will have the highest-growing share of consumer power in the region. The lesson for marketing specialists and those looking for future trends in identities and societal values is that, with the rapid pace of urbanization, the region likely will be dominated by members of the latter categories.

Table 4.1: Consumer Types in Five Arab Countries

Consumer Type	Algeria	Egypt	Jordan	Saudi Arabia	UAE
	(percentage of those surveyed)				
Religious conservatives	40	52	18	20	46
Societal conformists	40	22	36	19	13
New Age Muslims	7	20	34	47	17
Liberals	13	6	12	14	24

Source: Monita Vohra, Gagan Bhalla, and Aurobindo Chowdhury, "Understanding the Islamic Consumer," *Research World* (February 2000), 41.

It cannot be ignored that many Arabs, both Muslim and Christian, are religious, but this should not be equated with their being intolerant. In a 2010 Arab Barometer poll across the region, 61 per cent of respondents agreed or strongly agreed that "religion is a private matter and should be separated from sociopolitical life." There were considerable differences, however, across the nine Arab countries polled. The strongest support for religion's playing a role in socio-political matters was exhibited in Saudi Arabia, Yemen, Sudan, and the Palestinian territories, while the weakest support was exhibited in Egypt, Tunisia, Algeria, and Iraq.[10]

Arab youth also tend to be supportive of a strong role for religion in legal affairs, or *sharia* law. Most Arab Muslims supported the role of *sharia*, although Pew surveys find that, in a number of Arab countries, youth are less predisposed to support it – specifically, in Lebanon there is a 22 per cent differential between those who support *sharia* and those who do not; in Jordan and Tunisia, the difference is 12 per cent; in the Palestinian territories, the differential is 10 per cent.[11] Nevertheless, in a spring 2013 survey of 8,045 young Arabs between the ages of seventeen and thirty-one living in four countries that had gone through a revolution, there was strong support for *sharia* as the basis of future law, with 93 per cent of Libyan youth supporting *sharia*, 89 per cent doing so in Yemen, 64 per cent in Tunisia, and 57 per cent in Egypt.[12] *Sharia* law has been misconstrued in the West as suppressing minority rights or the imposition of a theocratic state on citizens. For many Arab

Muslims, however, *sharia* applies to personal matters such as inheritance, marriage/divorce, and property disputes,[13] and only in a few countries is it applied to military, political, or criminal cases. According to the Pew survey, Arab youth overwhelmingly favour democracy, but with a religious legal system in place. Squaring these two dimensions is, of course, the ongoing challenge, especially as there are few empirical cases to which one can point. After all, liberal democracy has yet to reach most Arab countries, and how to create both a tolerant society while preserving elements of *sharia* law is a matter worthy of public and legal debate, one I believe Arab youth are more willing and capable to discuss than ever before.

Nonetheless, the point remains: there is often a mistaken view, particularly among Western pundits, that those who identify as religious Muslims do not support democracy. In a poll of Arabs across the age spectrum, nearly 86 per cent supported democracy and were just about evenly split between those who wanted a secular democracy or a democracy that includes a role for Islam; only a small proportion of those surveyed supported a non-democratic secular system (6.3 per cent) or a non-democratic Islamic system (7.9 per cent).[14] From the same data set, Arab Barometer researchers found no correlation between a respondent's level of religiosity and support for democracy.[15]

The Better Half? Arab Women

The role of women in the Arab world has perplexed and infuriated outside observers. This is largely due to the conflicting ideas that exist – in the media, among ordinary citizens and activists, and even in official state reports and documents – about Arab women, particularly as these images and stereotypes exist in the West. Westerners often view Arab women as passive, exotic figures, with images of the Arab female ranging from the provocative belly dancer to the submissive female forced to wear a headscarf or the inscrutable *niqab* to the woman who is subject to draconian laws against everyday activities such as driving. As with all stereotypes, these have a veneer of truth, but they are nonetheless fleeting, distorted, and fractured impressions that do not represent the lived realities and perceived identities of women in the Middle East – or anywhere else for that matter. At the same time, there is no doubt that, despite (slowly) changing perceptions among youth, traditional views about women and work still exist throughout the Arab region.

A 2011 survey of 1,445 middle-class adults in Egypt, Saudi Arabia, and Morocco found that 59 per cent of young men between the ages of fifteen and twenty-four believed women should "be limited to housekeeping and child-care roles," compared with 80 per cent of men above the age of twenty-four. Ironically, answers to this question did not differ discernibly among adult men and women. Yet when young women between fifteen and twenty-four in the Gulf were asked about the role of women in the home, only 22 per cent agreed with the young men.[16] These findings indicate that there is a generational divide about the role of women in society and, at first blush, it appears that women are not being encouraged to work outside the home. However, in the same survey, 80 per cent said they believed a woman had the right to work outside the home and to pursue a professional career. Even in Saudi Arabia, perhaps the most conservative society of the Arab world, 94 per cent of these middle-class adult men in the survey believed that women should have the right to choose and pursue a career. In a 2005 poll of Arab men and women under age thirty, only a minority (16 per cent on average in six countries) believed it was "unacceptable for women to work," a response that was as low as 8 per cent in Lebanon and as high as 20 per cent in Saudi Arabia, with stronger support for women's right to work among female than among male respondents.[17] These surveys tell us that societal attitudes about women and work are changing in the Arab world, especially among the young and women themselves.

When Arab women in six countries were asked why they were unemployed, there were noticeable differences in the responses of the young (ages fifteen to thirty-five) and those of older generations. The most common reason, cited by 45 per cent, was a lack of opportunity to work; among older women, 43 per cent said they were unemployed because they needed to look after their children.

Family and spousal pressure not to work also differed across generations. Whereas 30 per cent of older women in the Gulf countries and 40 per cent of women in Jordan and Egypt responded that working was against the wishes of a family member or husband, only 14 per cent of younger women in the Gulf and 19 per cent of women in Jordan and Egypt concurred. Most interesting, across the six countries, only 3 per cent of young women said that, in their communities, it was "unacceptable for women to work," and even among older women (ages forty-nine to sixty-five) in the conservative Gulf countries, only 17 per cent agreed.[18]

These responses tell us a few things about perceptions of women and work in the Arab world worth noting. Undoubtedly, women as caregivers in the home are valued, and many women, as well as men, believe that raising children is an important priority. At the same time, young Arab women who want to work are challenging the societal norms that might have prevented their mothers' generation from doing so. The debate about whether women should stay home to raise their children and at what (if any) cost is not unique to the Arab region. Women, from the most progressive European countries to the conservative societies of the Arab region, have much to debate about how to balance a demanding family life, where the burden (or pleasure) of raising children too often falls on them, and to what extent they should expect help to do so. Needless to say, the Arab region, like many developing regions, has yet to provide the type of state support for maternity and paternity leave and daycare that makes these familial choices easier. That said, Arab family bonds are strong, and grandparents often help daughters and daughters-in-law juggle the demands of work and home.

Although Arab youth still have a generally conservative view about women and work, those I spoke to expressed more nuanced views that help illuminate the survey results noted above. Many of the young men, particularly from lower socio-economic classes, were not supportive of having their wives in the workforce unless it was necessary to meet the family's financial needs. According to Beshoy, a twenty-three-year-old cab driver in Cairo, "I want my future wife to concentrate on raising my children, but of course if we can't survive or give my children the lifestyle we want, then it is a good idea to have her work." The young men I interviewed repeated this sentiment often, especially if their future wives were likely to hold "pink collar jobs" – that is, employed in the services sector – or to work long hours in private sector companies that might also require lots of travel. But twenty-three-year-old Mohamed, a well-to-do medical student at Ain Shams University in Cairo, stated: "I would rather have my wife work and build a life together than continue to take money from my father to meet our lifestyle needs." Mohamed wants to marry a woman with a university degree who he expects will have a professional career: "Whereas, in my parents' generation, the wife was very dependent on her husband, today my female peers want to be independent and have a career. I like this because my generation want[s] to keep our independence while being married, by having our own circle of friends and not having to do everything together, which is very different than my parents' generation."

Indeed, as young people face the challenge of paying for an urban lifestyle full of modern, expensive amenities, inhibitions about women and work are eroding. For many Arab families, a double income has become not just a financial necessity, but a growing societal norm that is changing the dynamics of patriarchy throughout the Middle East. Nevertheless, the type of employment that women find remains a concern for many who continue to have conservative views about "preserving a woman's honour." These conservative views are more prevalent among lower socio-economic groups, those in poorer urban areas, and those in rural areas. Dana, a twenty-year-old female student at Yarmouk University in Jordan from a lower-middle-class family told me that most of the men in her peer group want to marry a woman who has a professional career, preferably in the public sector, where hours are light, there are few opportunities to travel, high job security, and a pension. Marrying a teacher, for example, is highly desirable. Dana told me that one place men look for a prospective wife is the newspaper, where, every year, the Jordanian Ministry of Education lists the names of newly appointed teachers. Men (and meddlesome mothers) then use this list to set up dates or meetings with these future teachers. Dana joked that even university yearbooks have become resources for nosy mothers who are looking for prospective wives for their sons, especially women who have graduated in the arts and social sciences and who likely will be employed in the public sector.

Beyond the debate about whether or not women should work is the reality that women increasingly are channelling their creativity into entrepreneurial activities. Compass, a US-based firm that tracks data on startups, found that, although the global average for female online entrepreneurs is 10 per cent, 35 per cent of online entrepreneurs in the Middle East are women.[19] In Egypt, women own 20 per cent of all firms, well above the developing world average, and are diversifying their businesses away from services to manufacturing[20] – for example, women own 45 per cent of Egypt's textile and clothing manufacturing companies. This is not to say that women in the Arab world do not face the challenges all women face – finding good child care, flexible work, secure financing, and so on – but, rather, that the image of the passive or submissive Arab woman simply does not fit with the current reality.

Arab women are challenging societal norms, and taking to online forums, television, and radio to get their voices heard. *Kalam Nawaem* is a free-to-air satellite TV program that is one of the most influential talk shows in the Arab world. It features four women from various professional and ideological backgrounds who sit and talk among themselves and with guests about current affairs and social issues. Akin to ABC's *The View*, *Kalam Nawaem* is popular among housewives and public personalities wanting to connect more with audiences of Arab women. The show is smart, analytical, and honest in tackling both hard and soft topics – everything from politics to cooking to marital relations – and represents a genre, an all-female cast, that simply was not seen on air in previous generations.

In the Arab region, traditional views about marriage and choosing a partner who is acceptable to one's social circle remain, but these are slowly changing among the young. In a survey of three thousand Arabs in nine countries, responses revealed that, of those not married, 46 per cent expected to make their own choices about whom they will wed.[21] That is still a very low proportion compared with Western norms, but family views about potential spouses are still important in the Arab world, and it might be that family input clouds the question of whether people really do make their own choice of a marriage partner. Young people in the Arab region are, however, increasingly deciding whom they will marry. Even in Saudi Arabia, the most conservative Arab country, surveys show that young people are more open now than ever before about whom they will marry and why. Surveys of Saudi youth in 2003 and again in 2011 found that, in less than a decade, support for marrying for love increased from 53 per cent to 64 per cent.[22] In a country where segregation of the sexes is common and there are few social places for men and women to meet and fall in love, the prevalence of such views is rather astounding. From conservative Saudi Arabia to liberal Lebanon, young Arab men and women are finding creative ways to meet, talk, and fall in love, and they are doing so with or without their parents' knowledge, often using technology to circumvent the social restrictions that were imposed on their parents' generation.

In my discussions with youth from all walks of life in the Arab world, I found that many had a strong desire and expectation to marry someone they love. The traditional approach to arranged marriage, where couples do not court each other and the parents decide, is quickly dying away, and seems to remain rooted in mainly underdeveloped rural areas. Zaina, a twenty-year-old Syrian engineering student who wears a colourful *hijab* and whose family sent her to study in Canada, reflected on her family's expectations of marriage: "Sure, my parents would love for me to marry a Syrian man and even preferably from our city of Damascus. But I'm smart and educated and I know if I argue with them, I can convince them that my choice is better. They'll change their mind." Almost all of the youth I spoke to expected to "date" or "get to know" their prospective partner for anywhere from a few months up to a year, and, in contrast to their parents' generation, most will meet and marry a person of their choosing. This will fundamentally change the marriage dynamics of young people. Indeed, one already sees new behaviour among young Arab couples with their children, including more fathers involved in parenting chores, more women actively engaged in the workforce outside the home, smaller families and higher use of contraceptives and family planning, and parenting styles that are less authoritarian and more authoritative with young children.[23] The change in parenting styles likely will produce a generation that is less rigid and absolute, and more creative, innovative, and socially tolerant.

Growing Up Cosmopolitan

Underlying all of this is the reality that the Arab world itself is becoming far more cosmopolitan, open, and inclusive. Many of the young people I met, particularly those in urban areas who are educated and hungry for social mobility, actually used the word *a'lami* (cosmopolitan) to describe their point of view. I was introduced to another term, "third culture kid, or TCK," by Melhem, a twenty-one-year-old financial analysis student from Syria who was studying in Canada. Melhem noted how he could adapt easily to both Western and Eastern cultures because he was a TCK. Other Syrian students in the same focus group nodded their heads in agreement that they, too, were TCKs. I later discovered that the term originated with a sociologist who observed that her children, who travelled frequently, adapted quickly to living in many different societies and actually felt "out of sync" when they moved back "home."[24] For many of the Syrian students I spoke to in Canada, the concept of home was quite fluid. According to Melhem:

> When people ask me what nationality I am, I say I am Syrian, because that is my passport. But I've never lived long in Syria. As a kid, we moved to Dubai, a very multicultural city where I saw more non-Arabs than Arabs. We visited Syria for [the] summers, but I do not really know a lot about life in Syria for locals. I might return "home" to build my country Syria after the war, but I now live in Canada, and life is good here too. I might stay and get a Canadian passport, but when I finish my studies, I know that I don't belong anywhere and yet can adapt to living anywhere.

In speaking to twenty-one-year-old Abdullah, a Syrian-born and -raised student who had never lived outside his native Aleppo until coming to study engineering in western Canada less than two years ago, I was surprised to find that he did not have the slightest accent in his pronunciation of English words. In fact, he spoke English fluently, and used all the idioms of any Western-born kid. At my prompting, Abdullah reflected on his views of the West and how they had changed after arriving: "We are so saturated with Western culture that coming from Syria to Canada was not a big transition for me. My professors and new friends in Canada keep telling me, 'wow, you look and dress like us,' or 'you are too liberal to be from the Middle East.' I hear that a lot. I think my presence of being an Arab guy in Canada was more of a cultural shock for the people I met here than it was for me to come to Canada. They didn't expect to meet a guy like me, but I expected everything that I have experienced here in Canada."

Whether Arab youth are TCKs or just able to see and hear Western culture with such ease, one gets the impression that they are more comfortable and open to Western culture than is so often assumed in popular discourse. When Arab youth in nine countries were asked, "How important is the idea of global citizenship – the shared feeling of identity regardless of ethnic, religious, or national background – to you?" 69 per cent believed it was important; only 15 per cent believed it was not important and another 16 per cent did not know. In the UAE, an increasingly multicultural country, 79 per cent agreed that global citizenship was important.[25]

In poll after poll, Arabs see no conflict between a modern society that embraces aspects of the Western rule of law and liberal democracy while leading a "religiously devout life."[26] Unlike previous generations that viewed Western and Islamic values as binary constructs, many Arab youth see the virtues and shortcomings of each society and want to blend the two in dynamic and innovative ways. Take *Khawater*, a highly respected and very popular MBC-TV show among Arab youth that has more than a million subscribers on YouTube. The host, Ahmed al-Shugairi, is a Saudi who uses his popular show to dispel myths about the "other" by showcasing the good and bad of modern life. Using hidden cameras and talking to people on the streets, he challenges misconceptions and highlights "virtuous" behaviour. In one popular episode, for example, a wallet is left unattended on a restaurant table in an Arab city and in Tokyo. The show filmed two contrasting videos, which showed that in most Arab countries people stole the wallet, while in Japan most people turned it in to local authorities. Breaking down popular misperceptions of other societies as immoral or decadent while highlighting the failure to uphold Islamic teachings in the Arab world is a signature of *Khawater*. Such self-criticism of Arab society and acknowledgment of the need to adopt positive aspects of Western society – particularly its emphasis on the rule of law – is becoming a prevalent theme in the culture. In an interview, Shugairi noted:

> The US, like any other nation, has a lot of positives and a lot of negatives. Something positive about the US is that it implements three Islamic teachings *more than most Arab countries*. The first is justice. In the United States, each individual has the right to go to court if he/she has been wronged. If a government official did something wrong, he will be held accountable and will be taken to court ... The second positive aspect of the US is another Islamic principle: reading, education, and seeking knowledge. People in the United States read, write, and publish books far more than in the Arab world. The West invents new technologies that teach and encourage people to read such as e-books and i-books. The third advantage in the US is freedom. This includes freedom of religion.[27]

Khawater contains many references to returning to Islamic principles of faith, which emphasize moderation, tolerance, good manners, and personal piety. Shugairi's popularity among Arab youth suggests a desire for a more cosmopolitan and inclusive interpretation of Islam, for bridging the gap between Western modernity and Islamic principles of dignity and social justice.[28]

Indeed, some of the most popular Arab programs on TV and online showcase the best of the West and East, and are slowly chipping away at the Arab establishment's use of binary constructs. On YouTube, *Sa7i*, another Saudi channel, tackles interesting social issues in comedic fashion. In one episode, the host of the show,

Ibrahim Salih, takes on the frustration of young males who are constantly asked to run errands and taxi around sisters and mothers who are not allowed to drive in Saudi Arabia. The video, which has attracted two and a half million views, teaches a poignant lesson about being a patient and respectful brother and son. Although not political, the message of the video is to show empathy and the need to tone down the bravado of Saudi males. And although Salih does not take on the overtly political issues of Saudi society, his social messages are among the most popularly viewed by young Saudis online.

Moreover, plenty of Saudi men are challenging state controls on women's freedoms. One YouTube video called "No Woman, No Drive," a play on the Bob Marley song "No Woman, No Cry," pushes for the revocation of Saudi laws forbidding women to drive. The music video was a sensational hit, with more than twelve million views, and was posted online by self-proclaimed artist, social activist, and stand-up comedian Hisham Fageeh on a day when Saudi women protested the ban on driving. The protests, both online and on the streets of Saudi Arabia, are youth-led movements that are pushing for social and cultural change. The youth involved are leading their generation and challenging the political and religious establishment one YouTube hit at a time. Many of these political activists have something else in common: they have been educated in the West, and are bringing this experience back home with them.

Conclusion

Arab youth hold a fusion of identities that do not fit the binary descriptions of their society. Tired of government narratives about the merits of secularism, curtailed rights to express their faith, and being treated as social threats rather than as social assets, Arab youth are calling for a new vision of social dignity and justice. Unlike previous generations, today's Arab youth are more apt to reject binary views of their identities as Western versus Eastern, secular versus religious, and individualist versus family-oriented. Instead, they are seamlessly mixing Eastern and Western values in their daily lives. They are increasingly cosmopolitan in their identities, well travelled, and conscious of the merits of adopting Western concepts of the rule of law and its institutions. They also see no contradiction in having both a liberal democracy and *sharia* law.

From choosing to marry a person they love to accepting the role of religion in society to rejecting the notion that Western ideals and institutions are foreign or unadaptable to Arab customs and culture, Arab youth hold values and identities that differ from those of their parents, and they will have a different life trajectory. Arab youth want immediate progress on the economic front, but they accept that political and social reforms might take longer to achieve. This should not be mistaken as their being in favour of the status quo; rather, they expect to usher in these changes and reforms themselves instead of relying on existing leaders. Demographic trends are on their side, and Arab youth have a vision of political and social change they want to bring about from the bottom up. As Arab youth increasingly intermix with peoples from around the globe, the influence of Western identities on the Arab region and the impact of Arab and Muslim identities on Western multicultural societies cannot be ignored. In the next chapter, I examine the increased transnational ties that bind the Arab and Western worlds, and how Arab youth increasingly are becoming the champions of these bonds, both contributing to and benefiting from the circular and global movement of people and ideas.

chapter five

Circularity

If you accept my premise that Arab society is changing from within – thanks to its youth, who are pushing it to become more competitive, accountable, and cosmopolitan – then you will also see that the "rise of the rest" to which I referred in the Introduction includes the Arab world. As the globe becomes increasingly interconnected via new social networks, rapid mobility, and new modes of exchanging ideas, Arab youth will participate and benefit in many, sometimes unexpected, ways. What will be the global impact of an educated, politically aware, and cosmopolitan Arab youth?

With increased transnationalism, the influences of the West in the Arab region and the impact of Arab and Muslim identities on Western societies cannot be ignored. After all, the Arab region is, as we have seen, a growing source of Western immigration. What is more, Arab students are flocking to learn in Western universities and, as I argue below, what these youth learn abroad and take home with them is a valuable part of understanding the future trajectory of their societies. An increasing number of Arabs now hold dual citizenship, particularly from Western countries, and Arab communities in Europe and the Americas are increasing the ties of these countries to the Arab region. These factors present opportunities in terms of promoting economic and cultural ties, but they also create challenges. Mutual understanding must be furthered, as does a greater awareness of how Arab perceptions of the West are informed by events and the policies of Western leaders.

Of the 350 million Arabs worldwide, 13 million are migrants, a high proportion of whom left in their youth. Forty-five per cent of the migrants have moved to other Arab countries, 38 per cent are in member countries of the Organisation for Economic Co-operation and Development, mostly France and the United States, and 18 per cent are in the rest of the world.[1] Arab migration exceeds the global average: whereas migrants account for 3.1 per cent of the global population, Arab migrants account for nearly 4 per cent of the Arab population.[2] If one includes both migrants and their descendants, the number of Arabs in these communities is reportedly as high as 37 million.[3] Western Europe now has a significant Arab population, estimated to be as high as 14 million; Brazil has as many as 12 million, many of whom are of Lebanese descent; and the United States has as many as 3 million. Nearly 40 per cent of France's foreign-born population is Arab, while Arabs account for between 11 and 15 per cent of the foreign-born populations of Spain, the Netherlands, Belgium, Italy, and Denmark.[4]

In this chapter, I argue that the Arab region's large émigré population of workers, talent, and students are agents of circularity who represent the lived experience of globalization. From an Arab regional perspective, transnational Arab youth should not be a viewed as a brain drain from Arab society, but as potentially providing a net benefit to the region in an increasingly globalized world. I argue that Arab youth who take advantage of circularity will remit not just money, but also important ideas and values that will shape the Arab region in the years to come.

From Immigration to Transnationalism

The history of Arab interaction with the world, particularly as merchants and traders, goes as far back as the earliest documentation of global trade. The Silk Road, for example, was one of the many trade routes that Arab merchants used to sell their spices and wares. When I visited the eastern terminus of the Silk Road in Xi'an, China, I was amazed to see the Arab influences on local cuisine and culture throughout its Muslim quarter, from all-spiced lamb to the dress and fashion of its Muslim minority. In more modern history, Arab communities in cities such as Buenos Aires, Montreal, New York, and Paris have also made their mark on local neighbourhoods. Narratives in literature and non-fiction chronicle the rich history of Arab communities abroad and their memories of home, challenges of settlement and assimilation, and evolving identities.

Until recently, the reality of settling in the West was a one-way trip for almost all waves of Arab migrants: returning "back home" or visiting friends and family in the "old country" was prohibitively expensive and time consuming. Yet, the pull away from home was a powerful one as people went in search of economic opportunity in Western countries.[5] To be sure, Arab youth who travelled from North Africa to Europe, from the Levant to the Americas and Australia, sought jobs in developed economies. The "return" was infrequent, and often only for special or sad occasions.

My father's immigration to Canada in the 1960s was just such a one-way trip, despite his thinking he would return home soon afterward. A young man in his early twenties, my father Fayiz first landed in Canada in the middle of a frigid winter. He vowed to return home at the first opportunity, only to discover that the next plane would not take off until the next season. When spring came, he changed his mind as he began to acclimatize both in spirit and in body to his new country. His short returns to his homeland were rare, once to marry my mother and another time to visit an ailing parent. For his first thirty years in Canada, his connection to the "home country" was weak. He rarely phoned home, and would save two weeks' pay to afford a quick call, which needed to be coordinated with his parents and siblings well in advance in order for them to get to their local postal station to receive his call. Sending letters by post took months, with little guarantee of delivery, so he had little regular connection to the family and friends he had left behind. Like many immigrants of his generation, my father integrated into Canada's social fabric and eventually lost connection with home. All he had left of his previous life was the memory of an Arab village frozen in time.

It would be mistaken to generalize about the experience of early Arab migrants to the West, but it seems fair to say that they were relatively successful and integrated well into their new homes. Many were Christian Arabs from Lebanon whose fair skin and religious background likely helped them to be received more warmly into a predominantly white, Christian society. Arabs in the Americas report higher-than-average incomes and, through circumstance as much as fortune, have not faced the same levels of racism as other groups, including Asians and Africans.[6] Moreover, Arabs in the United States and Canada are relatively more educated than the overall domestic population – 41 per cent of Arabs in the United States and 30 per cent in Canada have a university degree, compared with 24 per cent and 30 per cent of non-Arab Americans and Canadians, respectively.[7]

Arabs who arrived in the West after the 1980s, however, have not had the same experiences as earlier migrants. The rise and intensification of anti-Arab sentiment in the United States after the oil crises of the 1970s and 1980s, the events of 9/11, and the US interventions in Iraq both before and after 9/11, coupled with the increasing proportion of Arab migrants who are Muslim – and, consequently, more visible for those who choose Islamic-observant clothing – has meant that Arab-Americans today are more likely to face racism than before. In Europe, Arab migrants often originate from North Africa, are overwhelmingly Muslim, and have darker complexions than, say, Lebanese or Levantine Arabs, and face more open and intense forms of racism and lack of economic success than Arabs in the Americas.

For much of the twentieth century, Arabs living abroad often abandoned aspects of their ethnic identities to become acculturated into their new societies. In North America, Arabs often modified their names to fit in. Touring the Arab-American Museum in Dearborn, Michigan, I was struck by how many famous Arab-Americans were profiled and exhibited, yet few could be singled out as having Arab ancestry, as many had anglicized their names: Khouri became Corey, Zayed became Zed. For most Arabs living abroad, consciousness of their ethnic identity was relatively weak, as few reminders of the "old country" could be found or accessed in the West on a regular basis. Daily life for Arab migrants in the West, except for special occasions and holidays, provided little chance to experience their ethnic heritage, although food on family tables continued to keep its Arabic flavours.

Today, however, this model of one-way migration no longer applies as much as it did for my father's generation. We now live in a world characterized by "transnationalism," where people are interlinked in both the physical and virtual world in ways that blur borders and heighten economic, political, and cultural ties.[8] It is therefore useful to think of our world as a network with nodes and hubs that are mutually interdependent.[9] This means that, in our modern times, the movement of people is an added benefit to both the West *and* the Arab region. Arab youth are transmitters and beneficiaries of this movement to and through the West. As transmitters of circularity, higher numbers of Arab youth are studying and working in the West and increasing their economic, cultural, and political ties to the Arab region, irrespective of where they reside.

Undoubtedly, information and telecommunications technology, ease of transport, and greater mobility now allow Arabs to maintain emotional, financial, and cultural ties to their homelands. My newly immigrated cousin, Maha, feels as much at home in Toronto as she does in any Arab city. She can tune in Arabic channels via satellite and watch her favourite soap operas, cooking shows, and news programs. Around the corner, a grocer stocks all of the same brands and goods she purchases in the Middle East. When she misses her siblings and other relatives, she calls them on Viber or Tango and speaks to them for pennies, and keeps up with their news on Facebook. She maintains her social and cultural ties to the region, plans on visiting it on a regular basis, is currently considering investing in her brothers' businesses, and regularly sends money home to her parents. As a young professional who speaks Arabic and English fluently, she seeks job opportunities across the globe, including in the booming Gulf region. Economic, political, and social developments in the Arab region are of great concern to her, and she tunes in, participates in, and assesses news of her homeland as passionately as she would news about her new country. Her strong interaction with and ties to her homeland cannot compare to the isolation, loneliness, and resignation of no-return that my father felt towards his homeland in the 1960s. Whereas my father immigrated to Canada, my cousin is a transnational Arab whose "home" is in the Middle East as well as in Canada.

My cousin is like many of the growing number of Arab youth who live, migrate, or study in the West while keeping strong connections to their home countries. In a 2013 survey distributed to Arab-Canadian youth at a conference on professional development, I asked approximately a hundred attendees about their connection to the Arab region, the frequency of communication with it, and if they had participated in the Arab Spring.[10] Their responses confirmed what scholars of transnationalism have predicted: Arab youth in the diaspora are highly engaged in, care about, and participate in political, social, and cultural news of their home countries. Arab youth living in Canada are very connected to home, and tend to communicate with their countries of origin at least once a week, and to travel to the Arab region on average every two years. The most popular way Arab youth communicate with people back home is, perhaps not surprisingly, through Facebook, but this is closely followed by phone calls, texting, and Skype.

In addition to interacting and speaking with friends and family in their home countries, Arab youth regularly consume cultural and media products from the region. They listen to, read, and reflect on news broadcast from the Middle East with great interest, even more often than they tune into local and Canadian news. Generally once a week, Arab youth watch popular Arabic programs, music videos, or films on satellite television. They cheer for their favourite pop stars on *Arab Idol* and watch *Yalla NY*, a reality TV show that chronicles the lives of Arab youth trying to make it in New York City. Most important, Arab youth are politically engaged on issues that affect the Middle East. Nearly 85 per cent of the respondents to my survey said they had contributed in some way to the Arab Spring, by signing online protests or petitions, posting videos or images online, or tweeting, blogging, or participating in opposition movements against Arab governments. Surprisingly, 72 per cent said they had travelled, some to the Arab region itself, to participate in protests or demonstrations during the Arab Spring. In short, for Arab youth in the West, the ties to their home countries' political and cultural experiences are strong, and many are actively trying to participate in them and even shape them from abroad.

Arab Students in the West

According to the Institute of International Education, 52,648 Arab students travelled abroad during the 2011/12 academic year, a number that increased to 65,875 in 2012/13.[11] In any given year, more than a quarter of a million Arab students are abroad, completing their education in multiyear programs. Indeed, as a proportion of their respective populations, far more Arab youth than Chinese or Indian youth are studying in Western universities.[12] In 2012, Arab states sent about 901 students abroad per million population, while China sent 514 per million and India 156 per million; in terms of numbers, 321,418 Arabs, 694,365 Chinese, and 189,472 Indians were studying abroad in 2012.[13]

Thus, in impressively high numbers, Arab youth are living in Western countries to further their education. Their primary destination is the United States, followed by the United Kingdom. Also among the sought-after places in which to study are Canada, continental Europe, and Australia. These students come mostly from Kuwait, the UAE, Egypt, and, above all, Saudi Arabia, which in 2012 alone sent nearly 45,000 students abroad and currently has 160,000 students around the world, 90,000 of them in the United States. Many Saudi students are studying medicine or business, and most (75 per cent in 2011) are men, although the share of Saudi women abroad has increased dramatically over the years, and Saudi officials expect the share of females studying abroad under the King Abdullah Scholarship program to be at par with that of males in the coming years. That program, a competitive grant that commenced in 2005 and is expected to continue until at least 2020, is the most successful of the various scholarship programs established by Gulf governments since the mid-2000s. Recognizing that their oil-dependent economies require diversification and the human skills and capacity to compete in global markets, these governments are sponsoring students to learn and live abroad, and paying most of the expenses that students and their nuclear families incur.

These hundreds of thousands of Arab foreign students are bringing home more than just their postsecondary degrees. As one employee of a Gulf government, who chose to remain anonymous, told me, "They learn about equality, non-discrimination, and that everybody has all the same rights and privileges; something they don't learn and see if living in wealthy, nepotistic Gulf communities." The social and cultural impact of these returning Gulf students is thus having an affect on the values of their home countries, one that I believe is generally positive. The newly adopted values and ideas these students are taking home are what sociologists such as Peggy Levitt refer to as "social remittances."[14] Moreover, with the rise of social media, students and other Arabs living and working abroad have even more ways of injecting Western values, ideas, and liberal understandings of political culture into their home country societies.

In my many visits to the Arab region, I have seen the impact of these social remittances, and in meeting and talking with Arab students studying in Canada and the United States, I discovered a great deal about how they view their societies after having lived in both the West and the East. Ahmed, a Qatari now in his late twenties who had studied international affairs in the United States, told me about his experience:

I learned how to be open to other people's opinions. I became more independent and learned how to do things on my own. Having lived with Chinese, Indian, and other Arab students, I learned so much about other people's cultures. In Qatar, I would have never socialized with so many different cultural communities and learned about their societies. In Qatar, we are introverted and socialize only within our own socio-economic class and often look down upon foreign expats or manual workers living there. I finally really met and understood other cultures to see how we are so much alike. I now see how we need to change and improve things in Qatar.

As a professor of international affairs myself, I was curious to know what Ahmed took away the most from studying this topic in the United States. He said, "I finally saw the difference between politics as expressed by governments, and the values and sentiments of ordinary people. In the Arab world we assume a government's policies to be a reflection of its people, and I learned that this was wrong or at least shortsighted on my part."

I also met with a group of Syrian students who had left in the early days of the conflict in that country to pursue their studies in Canada. I started our discussion by asking them if they had experienced culture shock upon coming to Canada. They all shook their heads and said they had no problems transitioning to Western life. Saudi students, like the Syrians, had also adjusted quickly to life in Canada. Omar, a twenty-six-year-old engineering student, told me: "Before I left Saudi, I already knew a lot about the city of Waterloo [Ontario]. I used YouTube to see videos of other students and Waterloo residents, so I had a sense of what was going on here. I even used Google Maps, so by the time I arrived in the city I knew how to get around and where things were." A business student, nineteen-year-old Fahd, added: "It is true that we don't have any difficulty in functioning in the West, but the hardest thing for me was to have to work with female students or interacting with them in a classroom. In Saudi, we are segregated, and this was the first time I had to work in group projects with female students." To be sure, despite their need to adapt to a few of the more challenging aspects of life abroad, as Fahd's experience illustrates, many of the male Saudi students nonetheless suggested that the transition to life in the West was not as abrupt and shocking as they had expected.

I asked both the Syrian and Saudi groups of students about the ideas and practices they would most likely want to take home with them from the West. Many responded that multiculturalism was the best lesson or idea the West had to offer the Arab region. Dawood, a twenty-five-year-old Saudi engineering student, reflected on this: "Now, living in the West, without my family, I'm so homesick. I really wish that they could be here with me as I study. They have visited me in Canada, and I really appreciated that they could come to see me. I think back to all the Pakistani workers in Saudi who were not allowed to bring their families with them and I now see how this is so unfair. We should change Saudi rules to allow foreign workers to bring families with them." Omar added:

On my last trip leaving Saudi Arabia, I saw a Saudi border agent discriminate and be rude to a Pakistani worker coming into the country. At the time I stayed quiet and didn't think of it, because it is so common to look down upon minorities who come to work in Saudi. Then I arrived in Canada and felt the same way when a border agent looked at me, with my beard and Saudi dress, and realized she was looking down at me, the same way we Saudis look at the Pakistani workers. This agent was also not welcoming and [was] unkind in her tone and questions. Wow, I now knew how this Pakistani worker, who is just trying to better his life, feels. I will never let that happen again. Next time I'm in Saudi and I see this discrimination, I'm going to stand up for these workers.

Many of the Saudi students I spoke to talked about the respect that Western societies seemed to have for minorities, and viewed it as a positive attribute that they want to practise when they returned home. The Syrian students were also impressed with the value of multiculturalism and the notion of equality before the law. Zaina, a twenty-year-old engineering student whose family sent her to study alone in Canada, talked about how she appreciated the fact that Canadians did not seem to care about whether you were rich or poor, a member of a minority group, or what family you came from.

The Syrian and Saudi students also said that their experience in the West had taught them renewed respect for the environment, law enforcement, community centres, and investment in public spaces and public transport. They were especially vocal about how respect for the environment was sorely lacking and desperately needed in the Arab region. As Abdullah, a nineteen-year-old science student stated: "We have to change in Saudi and start teaching our kids from a young age about keeping our country beautiful. Not to throw garbage on the street and wait for a cleaner to pick it up. Things in the West are so neat and organized, and clean. We can do the same in Saudi if we focus on keeping our country clean." Hashim, a twenty-one-year old engineering student said that, when his family came to Canada to help him begin his studies, the first thing they did that was out of the ordinary for them was to use the trash bins in the airport. I asked the groups what they would do differently when they got home. Zaina replied, "When I go back to Syria, I won't throw garbage on the street anymore. I just won't do this. It has become the norm for me." The other Syrian students in the group nodded in agreement. Similar sentiments were shared by the Saudi students. According to Fahd, for example, "I love being able to separate my garbage into recyclables and biodegradables. This is so amazing. When I get married, I'm going to teach my kids about recycling. Even if it costs me more to put in practice into my home, I want my kids to value and appreciate having a clean country."

Many of the students also appreciated public transport. Omar, for example, noted: "I still can't believe that an entire bus full of so many people would stop for me to get on. I feel embarrassed by how amazing it is that an entire bus would stop for just one person. In Saudi, people use their cars to get everywhere, but public buses are not just cleaner for the environment, but they also build a community. On the bus, I look around and see we are all different races and religions. When I'm on the bus, I feel like we are all one family, working together."

The young Arab students studying in the West whom I spoke to were also enthusiastic about the value of Western laws. Whereas, in Saudi and Syria, for example, a parking infraction could be dismissed with the help of family networks or tribal connections, the significance of all people being equal before the law was something they regarded as an inherent feature of a modern society. Omar recounted one example of the wonders of having established law enforcement: "I got a parking ticket the other day, and thought how amazing this was. Ironically, I felt like this is what we need most in Saudi: law enforcement … I won't park in an illegal spot again." In his focus group, Melhem also commented on the great respect Westerners have for pedestrians: "I love the fact that pedestrians have the priority. In Damascus, I have no priority as a pedestrian and could easily get run over. I also think it is great that there are no sounds of car horns throughout the city here. In Damascus, people honk for no reason and are rude drivers. I like the structure [of things] here better, and it comes from respecting other people. I probably say thank you and sorry more here than I ever said in the Middle East."

Most of the Arab students I spoke to wanted to return to their home countries. Listening to the experiences of these students, it became clear that, in small and, at times, seemingly insignificant ways, they will make a notable impact on their societies. Indeed, given the current rise of disputes and communal violence among ethnic and religious groups throughout the Arab world, the promotion of multiculturalism – in particular, its celebration of diversity, equality, and tolerance – by Western-educated young Arabs upon their return home is likely to make a valuable and, one hopes, sustainable contribution to the Arab region.

In speaking to a number of Saudi women studying abroad, I sensed a particularly strong feeling of pride in wanting to use their educational skills upon returning home. They reflected positively on the many social and political values they had learned in the West, but they were also cognizant of the challenges they would face at home. Amal, for example, was studying in Canada to be an obstetrician. I asked her if she was looking forward to returning to Saudi Arabia. Amal was frank: "My government has invested a lot of money in my education here in Canada. I know I got an excellent education, but it might be all a waste. Once I go back to Saudi Arabia, I won't have the money to hire a driver, and if I don't have a driver, I can't be on call to deliver babies! Not being able to drive means that I'm useless as an obstetrician! I would prefer to stay in Canada, but I'm committed to go back to Saudi."

Two young Saudi women, Rasha and Sarah, who returned to the Kingdom after studying in England were featured in a government-owned English-language newspaper, the *Saudi Gazette*. They lamented about how much easier it was for them to be mobile and independent in England. Rasha, who studied media at University of Leicester, noted: "The difficulty of women paying bills, for example, unless you are with a male guardian, is immense. A few days ago Mobily [a Saudi mobile company] refused [me to] go in and pay for my Internet subscription unless a male guardian was with me."[15] Similarly, Sarah, who studied psychology in Birmingham, added: "I still find it difficult to complete my day-to-day activities conveniently without the need of a driver. It can be really hectic if you don't have one. Not having a car was never an issue [in England]. Public transportation was everywhere and very easy to use."[16] Indeed, for most Saudi women, mobility is severely constrained. Many rely on male guardians to move safely from one place to another; the more affluent hire drivers. My impression is that most Saudi women living abroad feel conflicted about returning home, perhaps on account of experiencing a legal system that gives them complete liberty of movement.

An exception to those Saudi female students who would not challenge Saudi cultural practices outwardly is a young woman I met named Loujain, from a large and well-known Saudi tribe. Now twenty-five, Loujain spent many years studying abroad, first in France and then in Canada. Like many Saudi women studying abroad under the King Abdullah Scholarship program, living in the West she was exposed to the simple freedom of mobility that is not available at home. Loujain did more than just quietly protest; she recorded herself driving her own car, while not wearing a *hijab*, and posted the video online. The video, which has been viewed over three million times, garnered much uproar for overtly defying Saudi laws and mores. Taking up the challenge of Saudi critics who called her out for driving in Canada while "dangerously" encouraging women to do so in Saudi Arabia, upon returning to Saudi Arabia she filmed herself driving from the airport to her family home. Her act of defiance stirred further debate and, more important, helped spur national driving campaigns by fellow Saudi female activists. As she told me in our interview, Loujain believes that she "brought a little bit of hope to other Saudi women." I doubt, however, that she is finished making an impact on her society.

Indeed, what effect will these educated women have on conservative Saudi culture after studying in the West? One thing seems certain: an unintended consequence of the Saudi scholarship program will be to change existing attitudes about women's place in Saudi society as tens of thousands of educated women who have experienced life in the more liberated West return home to put pressure on the Saudi government to ease current restrictions on women's movement throughout society.

The Brain Circulation of Arab Youth

According to the 2009 Arab Knowledge Report, "[t]he Arab region is considered one of the most active in terms of the export of highly qualified human capital equipped with university degrees. Indeed, human capital is among its major exports, possibly equaling oil and gas in value."[17] Although this is perhaps an overstatement, it serves as a reminder that Arab people are an important part of the conversation about migration, mobility, and circularity.

The emigration of Arab labour – the "brain drain" of skilled Arab migrants who sought work and better economic opportunities abroad – was once seen as a net loss for Arab societies. Flows of people, money, and talent went from "the rest to the West." Egypt, in particular, saw its most gifted engineers, scientists, and educated young people migrate to the West to take up prominent industrial posts and academic positions. Among those who were part of the Arab diaspora that migrated to the West in the 1960s and 1970s were two Egyptians who later won the Nobel prize: Ahmed Hassan Zewail in 1999 for chemistry and Mohamed ElBaradei in 2005 for peace. Today, however, Arab youth, like my cousin Maha, who leave their home countries to work and earn better incomes remain closely connected to their home countries – in effect transforming the "brain drain" into a "brain circulation." Like the Indian migrants working in Silicon Valley who returned to Bangalore and developed its vibrant information technology economy, Arab migrants, whether permanent or temporary, bring back knowledge, capital, experience, and professional networks that benefit their home countries.[18] They also send home a great deal of money.

In Egypt, for example, remittances by the large number of workers abroad accounted for US$6.4 billion over the period from 2000 to 2010, or 4.4 per cent of the country's gross domestic product (GDP) per annum – more income than Egypt received from the Suez Canal (US$4.2 billion, or 2.9 per cent of GDP, in 2014). A high proportion of these remittances – 34 per cent of the total in 2008 – come from the United States, where, although the number of Egyptian expatriates is relatively small, they are generally highly educated and likely have dual nationality. In 2008, 22 per cent of remittances came from Egyptians working in the Gulf countries – 83 per cent of Egyptians working abroad do so in the Gulf, mostly in Saudi Arabia – but these are generally less educated and hold temporary work contracts.[19]

How countries use migrants' and workers' remittances for local development is of considerable debate. Early migration studies assumed that remittances were used solely to meet the consumption needs of families and individuals at home, and although a high proportion is still used for this purpose, an increasing amount is being diverted to invest in education, real estate, and small enterprises.[20] Egyptians working abroad, for example, increasingly are saving and sending money home to start new business ventures. If and when these migrants return home, they are more likely than non-migrants to become entrepreneurs and to earn higher wages or to help family members do so. Given the ease of transferring money and improved communication between migrants and their homes, families, business partners, or other contacts, Egypt is experiencing the positive flows of "brain circulation."[21]

Migration abroad to earn money is, in fact, the desire of a significant proportion of Egyptian youth. In a national survey of fifteen thousand youth ages fifteen to twenty-nine, 18.4 per cent – 29.7 per cent of males and 6.7 per cent of females – said they wanted to migrate.[22] Most wanted to go to the oil-rich Gulf, but of those who wanted to go to the West, more were from urban areas than from rural areas.[23] Besides Egyptians, large numbers of Arabs emigrate from the Maghreb countries of Morocco, Algeria, and Tunisia, mostly to Europe to study and work. As French speakers, their primary destination is France, the former colonial ruler of these countries. One study found that nearly 30 per cent of Algerian migrants who returned home and 20 per cent of Tunisians and Moroccans who did so became entrepreneurs.[24]

I had the opportunity to meet with talented Moroccans who, after studying or working in France for several years, opted to return to work in Morocco – the Bank al-Maghrib, Morocco's central bank, for example, actively recruits talented economists and financial analysts among the large Moroccan diaspora. The bank, along with the booming Moroccan private financial services and management consulting sector, conducts annual trips to cities with large Moroccan immigrant communities, such as Montreal, Amsterdam, and Paris, to recruit new talent. In coordination with head-hunting firms and Moroccan embassies abroad, these job fairs have successfully attracted some of the most talented Moroccans working for foreign companies outside the country to return to Morocco. I met with Mohamed, for example, who studied in France and then worked in a private French bank for nearly a decade before being lured back to work at Bank al-Maghrib when the global financial crisis hit Europe in 2008. Mohamed and others like him who are looking for success and upward mobility are open to job opportunities in both his adoptive France and his home country.

The third-largest number of Arab migrants are Palestinians, Jordanians, and Syrians, who head mostly to the Gulf states. Most stay for decades, then return to their native country to retire or to send their adult children to university. Here, of course, Palestinians are the exception given that those who leave occupied territories after a few years also lose their "right of return." Still, many have returned, or expect to return, at least to Jordan, where some of them hold citizenship.

For many Arab youth, their preference is to find work in the dynamic and booming UAE, which is attracting educated professionals from all over the world, particularly in the lucrative economic sectors of engineering and architecture.[25] In my travels in the UAE, I met a young married couple, Ahmed and Manal, two classmates who migrated from Jordan to live and work in Abu Dhabi. They claimed that half their engineering class from Zarqa University in Jordan had migrated to the Gulf to work. I asked them about their reasons for moving to the Gulf. Twenty-seven-year-old Manal replied: "Life is easy here. It is more organized than Jordan. I like all of the modern amenities here, and the fact that we are equal before the law. People are more respectful of the law here, partly because the Emirati have zero tolerance for bad behavior by any expat and we can all be deported easily. But for me, as a professional engineer with a young family, this is perfect. We have stability, prosperity, and safety here. I like it, but it is not home." I asked Manal's husband, Ahmed, also twenty-seven but a Palestinian, to reflect on why he chose to come to the UAE and whether he felt his rights as a non-citizen meant he was more vulnerable. He replied: "For Palestinians and Jordanians, we don't feel that we have more or less rights here in the UAE, compared to, say, Jordan where I came from. As long as we are respectful of the law, we live a really good life. Salaries are better, and we can save money to return to Jordan and either start a business or retire nicely. We never feel that Abu Dhabi will be our home. There is also a constant reminder by local Emirati that you are just a guest worker. And for me, that is ok, because this is not home for us."

Manal's and Ahmed's views were similar to those of other expatriate Jordanians, Syrians, and Palestinians I spoke with in the UAE, almost all of whom were highly educated professionals. This is not to say that there is not another story to be told of millions of South Asian and Egyptian workers in the Gulf and Saudi Arabia, many of whom work in unskilled jobs and who have experienced hardships that some have criticized as being little more than indentured labour.[26] Nevertheless, for educated Arab youth who travel to the Gulf to work, the experience can be positive. That said, as non-citizens, their status remains, at times, precarious.

What stands out in my conversations with expatriate Arab youth living in the Gulf is their outlook on the policies of their home countries. Many spoke of how Gulf governments spend money on their societies in generous ways. Undoubtedly, this is attributable to the fact that Gulf governments generate a great deal of revenue from state-owned oil exports and facilities, and typically spend some of the money on their relatively small populations (an exception is relatively populated Saudi Arabia), whereas many non-Gulf Arab countries, Algeria and Libya aside, do not have oil resources, but have much larger populations to support. To be sure, many of the Arab youth I spoke to were critical of their home governments for not spending on youth programs, education, and infrastructure in the manner they have seen Gulf governments spend. Some believed, rightly or wrongly, that, compared to their home countries, there is a greater distribution of wealth in the Gulf that promotes economic development there. They were also aware that things worked more smoothly, in an organized and modern sense, in the Gulf, while their home governments did not put in the same effort.

Listening to an interview with Wael Ghonim, the now-infamous Google executive who started the "We are all Khaled" campaign on Facebook to expose policy brutality in Egypt, one gets a sense of how Arab youth feel about living in the Gulf. In one of his most influential interviews with Dream TV in the midst of the Egyptian Revolution, he talked about his life as an Egyptian working in the UAE and his yearning to come home. Reflecting on the moment when, in prison, a police officer had called him a traitor, Ghonim noted:

> We [imprisoned activists] love Egypt! If I was a traitor I would have stayed by the swimming pool in my house in the UAE, have fun, and enjoy my life, get paid, every once in a while my salary increases. There's no problems. Should I say what others are saying? Let [Egypt] burn! Is it our country? It's theirs! That's what I'd say if I was a traitor. We're not traitors! Thank God, one of the things I'm proud of is that I went home knowing that I convinced these people that we're not traitors. I know what I'm saying and I know they are now convinced that the only motive we had [as protestors] was our love for our country.[27]

Like many Arab expatatriates, Ghonim expressed his desire to take the best of what the Gulf life has to offer and to apply it back home. As we have seen in this chapter, the remittances young Arab professionals send home include not just money, but ideas about the virtues of law and order, the merits of a multicultural society, meritocracy, and the role of government in spurring economic opportunity.

Conclusion

The image of the world today as interconnected, with hubs and nodes where people of different ethnic, cultural, and religious backgrounds traverse the globe, has at times, perhaps understandably, been seen through a kind of utopian lens. Yet one cannot ignore the reality that most citizens of the world do not have the legal and economic means to just pack up and go to another society. After all, travel and mobility depend on what governments and their border security deem to be the right or wrong passport. Western borders are not open to everyone; rather, they welcome people from select countries and socio-economic classes. As a professor, I often find myself in social circles composed of people who speak of travelling the globe, who share stories of the best restaurants in this or that capital, and who give advice on avoiding overrated hotels in this or that city. Undoubtedly, this is an elite world open to a small minority, not to one and all.

And yet I cannot help but reflect on the reality that cities around the globe are becoming more diverse and multicultural. Notwithstanding the elitist and discriminatory nature of global migration, the Arab region and Arab youth are increasingly connected to other societies in a way that opens new possibilities for the transnational diffusion of norms and values about politics, economics, and community. I believe that this is all for the better, and reason for added hope and optimism about the region.

The Arab world has always been a tapestry of diverse cultures, religions, and ethnicities, and to see Arab youth take home the merits and values of multiculturalism gives me much hope for the region's minorities. Yet the region still faces significant problems of intolerance. In the final chapter, I discuss what to make of the rise of violence and extremism by a small minority, as undoubtedly this is on the minds of many in the West when they think of the Arab world.

chapter six

Conclusion

By 2030 Arab countries must create 94 million new jobs, roughly 5 million per year, just to avoid increasing already high unemployment rates. Equipped with a growing consumer base of young people who are highly educated, but who make up a relatively inexpensive workforce, Arab countries are yearning for human and capital investment. Arab governments must innovate, promote entrepreneurship, and channel investment into labour-intensive sectors. Throughout my travels in the Arab region, I encountered a desire for productive and meaningful jobs – it is no coincidence that youth in Tahrir Square shouted "bread," a simple word evoking economic opportunity.

Although Arab youth are increasingly educated, the bane of unemployment has larger consequences for their life trajectory and for the region's future. As Dhillon, Dyer, and Yousef aptly note in their chapter in the book *Generation in Waiting*, as they move into adulthood, youth build their lives around the four pillars of education, employment, marriage, and housing. Without productive jobs, they cannot meet traditional marriage expectations, provide for a family, or afford suitable housing.[1]

The Imperative of Job Creation

Responsibility for job creation in the Arab region largely falls to government. Although Arab governments are typically no different

in size than those of other developing nations, they play a significant role in creating a constructive policy environment for both the
public and private sectors. It is an immense, but not impossible,
task: policies designed to capitalize on the "demographic dividend" of Arab youth exist. Governments can foster such an environment by scaling up the value of their educated youth workforce,
by investing in skills formation, and by tailoring education curri-
cula to work in tandem with the needs of the market. That said,
governments should not value or premise economic success solely
on rising macroeconomic indicators such as growth of gross domestic product (GDP), but also on the increased productive capacity and employment of society, or "inclusive growth."[2] Although
legislating a minimum wage to protect vulnerable sectors is not a
policy recommendation that economists with international organizations often cite, Arab governments would be wise to consider it.

Dhillon, Dyer, and Yousef recommend that Arab governments
expand the role of the private sector to steer youth away from
seeking government employment. They also urge the creation of
more human capital by improving the quality of education and
increasing university admissions and training initiatives, especially for marginalized groups such as women. As well, the authors
suggest that Arab governments involve youth in decision-making
and use fiscal stimulus policies to help youth find employment.
The authors also note the need to reform public sector hiring practices, to raise the value of informal jobs through investment in
skills development, and to improve job information and counsel-
ling. In the long run, they say, Arab countries need to work towards providing social security for all workers.[3]

The quest to improve employment success begins with responding to the needs of private sector employers by focusing on
promoting writing, critical thinking, and problem-solving skills.
Arab countries have introduced a number of recent initiatives to
build private-public partnerships to enhance the quality and relevance of education. A region-wide initiative called Injaz, for example, is "a partnership between Ministries of Education and the
private sector that gets business leaders to teach marketable skills
to high school and college students, including basic business skills,

teamwork, leadership skills, and entrepreneurial thinking."[4] Such initiatives need to be scaled up, however, to maximize their impact. Moreover, Arab governments and societies need to encourage critical thinking not just in the workplace but in the public space as well. Giving youth the opportunity to choose their cell phone provider or what pop star to vote for on *Arab Idol* is not sufficient. Governments need to recognize that the voice of youth in politics, issues of accountability, and social rights also needs to be appreciated and cultivated.[5]

Across the Arab region, governments are playing a key role in managing the task of creating jobs, but the public sector alone clearly cannot meet the demands for employment by the large volume of youth graduates. Instead of trying simply to absorb new labour market entrants, governments should focus more on creating an environment that is welcoming to investors and labour-seeking firms. For example, despite some structural reforms, Arab economies continue to lag in their efforts to attract foreign investment. Indeed, of total international foreign investment, only 1 per cent goes to Arab countries, which account for only about 2 per cent of the share going to developing countries.[6] This suggests that there remains an untapped opportunity for Arab governments to attract and retain international investment. This is less of a concern in the oil-producing Gulf states, whose capacity to take in foreign capital is lower and where national savings, or capital surplus in the economy thanks to oil exports, are already high. In the non-oil-producing Arab countries, however, national savings are lower and the need for injections of external capital is high. Arab governments, particularly outside the Gulf, need to attract foreign investment not just to create jobs, but also to acquire potential ancillary benefits such as technology transfer, access to research and development, international supply and distribution chains, and, under the right conditions, gain from added economic growth.

That said, in some parts of the Arab region, particularly outside the Gulf, the policy environment is not yet conducive to increasing international investment. The sad fact is that this inability stems primarily from pervasive corruption, particularly at the elite and government level, which discourages foreign investment, particularly the kind that requires assurances if the investor is to make a long-term, fixed commitment. Arab countries thus should not be enchanted by foreign firms that want to come into the region with a short-term strategy to make money through carry trade, and purchases of government bonds and fungible assets that give little indication of investor confidence. Foreign investors also have a responsibility not to perpetuate government corruption, human rights violations, and environmental degradation. Too often, Arab governments have used foreign investment as a global seal of approval of their system of poor governance. This will not be tolerated in a world where Arab youth have access to information and a network for sharing the facts. Improving transparency by publishing data on finances, spending, and public investment would go a long way to helping curb corruption. Here, international agencies have a positive role to play. In a meeting I had with an Arab central banker, for example, she confessed that one of the merits of her country having an International Monetary Fund (IMF) arrangement was that it forced internal bureaucratic agencies to get the numbers to balance correctly across entities, which highlighted their governance shortcomings and helped expose corruption.

In conjunction with increasing international investment in the Arab region, increased integration with international markets could be the key to unleashing output and labour demand. Evidence suggests that increasing Arab countries' openness to the level of emerging market economies in Asia could raise the region's annual per capita GDP by a full percentage point.[7] Ultimately, increased liberalization will be crucial for Arab countries if they are to diversify trade with rapidly emerging markets. With Europe's economy apparently slowing as a result of its aging population, the Arab region should foster closer ties with Africa and Asia, where economic growth continues and some complementarity of trade exists.

Some Arab countries, however, lack the capacity to create good, productive jobs, and also face the challenge of matching skills with the needs of the domestic and regional economy. The migration of youth throughout the region and to Western economies is useful to release pressure, but it cannot replace the need for better policymaking. Arab governments also need to improve the capacity and incentives to capture workers' remittances as well as to attract investment from the Arab diaspora. For many diaspora communities in the West, however, the bureaucratic red tape involved in starting a business in their home countries dissuades such investment. Arab governments could help overcome these difficulties by using their embassies abroad as one-stop shops for interested investors.

Labour-rich countries such as Egypt, Saudi Arabia, and Morocco should focus on strengthening their agricultural sector with more government investment, and promoting non-agricultural work in rural areas, which are too often neglected and their productive value to the economy discounted – a short-sighted strategy that spurs slum-dwelling in cities. Egypt and Morocco could also use their abundant labour and unique geographic positions to promote and court manufacturing firms. Morocco has already taken an important step in this direction by concluding a free trade agreement with the United States. Its success in exporting goods ranging from textiles to automobiles is a lesson for other countries in the region, particularly Egypt. Tunisia, with a relatively small population, has also been successful in promoting its textile sector by expanding beyond production to include fashion, design, and upgraded weaving and textile manufacturing.[8] For the rest of the Arab region, however, the kinds of low-skill manufacturing sectors that Asian countries and parts of Latin America have already carved out successfully are no longer an option. With increased protectionism taking place outide regional trading blocs, many Arab countries are too late to enter into competition with industrializers that have carved advantages, both trade and non-trade, to boost their manufacturing sectors.This is partly because of increased protectionism, which makes it more difficult for late-entry industrializers. As well, most Arab countries also have small populations and lack the comparative advantage to create successful manufacturing sectors. In any case, as Arab youth become more educated, they will prefer high-skilled jobs over low-skilled ones.

Policy Proposals for Productive Job Creation

Among the more promising sectors in the Arab region – that is, sectors that can make use of the talent of educated Arab youth and that are needed for economic growth – are finance, banking, infrastructure, telecommunications, engineering, oil and gas, and hospitality and tourism. This is by no means an exhaustive list, but the potential value-added benefits of further investment in these sectors and what they mean for Arab youth are significant.

Arab stock markets have become a "new frontier" – headlined, for example, in the *Wall Street Journal* – for both economic exploration and investment.[9] Granted, these stock markets are still greatly underdeveloped, but they offer attractive opportunities for portfolio diversification and optimization, which in turn can signal promising growth sectors.[10] As regulatory changes are put in place, a number of Arab stock markets are attracting the interest of international investors – one market index provider has already upgraded the stock markets in the UAE and Qatar from frontier status to that of an emerging market economy.[11] The liberalization and development of the Saudi stock market is also allowing foreign investors to enter lucrative markets in that country. Other countries, such as Tunisia, are trying to open the stock market beyond individuals to include institutional investors such as insurance companies.[12] These developments in regional stock exchanges suggest that this sector and related spinoff industries and firms offer opportunities for new jobs that can absorb and attract Arab talent. Brokers, investment houses, security specialists, asset managers, wealth specialists, accountants, economists, and market analysts are increasingly in demand throughout the region thanks to this burgeoning economic sector.

To develop Arab stock markets, the region also needs to grow its banking sector. This, however, will require changes in existing attitudes. Arab governments should reform macroeconomic policy and financial institution regulations to encourage individuals to save and invest and to create healthy competition in the banking sector. The conventional banking sector is improving, but competition remains low, foreign banks are generally unwelcome, the lack of bankruptcy laws prevents risk taking in the private sector, and small and medium-sized enterprises face difficulties accessing financing, particularly outside the Gulf.[13] The IMF notes there is ample capital available in the region, but the lack of competition among banks means that loans are hard to get; as well, rigid lending rules favour large firms.[14] Still, the expansion of Islamic banking during the 1980s and 1990s has allowed what was once a niche market to develop into a key sector throughout the Arab region. The sector is growing rapidly – by nearly 20 per cent since the 2008 global financial crisis – and is expected to remain on this trajectory until 2018.[15] Already, with more than three hundred Islamic banks and investment houses spread across more than seventy-five countries around the globe, the sector manages an amount that, in 2015, could reach US$4 trillion.[16] Islamic banks – governed by *sharia* law – do not charge interest, and are therefore less susceptible to the kinds of gyrations that affect the global financial system. Moreover, Islamic banks do not buy into the types of assets and financial instruments that are prone to speculative attacks or not based on solid tangible assets. This has proved to be a welcome and innovative solution to complement conventional, interest-based banking throughout the Arab region. According to one IMF study, "[b]ecause Muslim populations [have underdeveloped banking infrastructure], and given the tremendous need for infrastructure projects like roads and housing across the Muslim world, development of Islamic banking can spur growth in these regions, and can be part of the solution to the slow development process."[17] Islamic banking thus can serve both regional and global needs for diverse assets and investments, meaning, in turn, that Arab youth are well placed to fill jobs in banking, consulting, accounting, finance, legal services, and international negotiations.

Infrastructure could also be an important source of jobs in many Arab countries. In some areas, such as the Gulf states, public infrastructure is already modern and developed, but in other countries, such as Yemen and Sudan, it is sorely lacking. The entire region has a great need for such infrastructure as water desalination and management projects, mass transit, electricity, railways, modern ports and logistics, affordable housing, education, and health care facilities. Improving infrastructure could also improve labour market efficiencies. Too often, for example, women are not active participants in the labour market because they cannot access transportation that is safe and reliable. Indeed, transportation was a serious concern for many of the young educated women I spoke to throughout the Arab region. Rural women, in particular, might be highly educated and have job opportunities in cities, but socially conservative cultures prevent them from living alone in cities or taking crowded and impractical public transit.

According to the IMF, spending an extra 1 per cent of GDP on infrastructure could yield an additional eighty-seven thousand jobs in Egypt and eighteen thousand in Tunisia.[18] Not all governments can afford to invest in these public goods, but these sectors are well suited to public-private partnerships, which could ease the fiscal burden of the "megaprojects" some governments have undertaken.[19] When implemented with proper institutional frameworks – in areas such as leveraging domestic financing, ensuring open and transparent bidding and evaluation processes, providing a robust legal and regulatory framework, and fostering public participation in planning and decision-making – these projects could inject much-needed revenue into local economies and meet the needs of the wider public. They could also employ talented Arab youth in a variety of jobs, including high-skilled work in engineering, management, architecture, urban planning, surveying, and legal services, to name a few.

Public-private infrastructure development can boast of some success stories – such as the Abu Dhabi Water and Electricity Authority and the Oman Power and Water Procurement facility – but the region could benefit greatly from more of these types of projects. With its growing population, the region will experience increased demand for public services such as electricity, power, water, and transport. Countries with surplus capital, such as the Gulf oil exporters, would be well advised to support and co-finance large infrastructure projects in the region. The malls, office towers, resort villages, and other luxury developments that Gulf developers often finance are not a long-term development strategy that will serve a youthful population, but investment in public infrastructure projects could be quite lucrative both economically and diplomatically for Gulf investors. Indeed, the point here is that *both economic and political resolve* are needed to ensure that infrastructure development succeeds.

The Arab region is also home to some of the world's most important reserves of oil and natural gas, and refining and resource exploration provide useful job opportunities for Arab youth. The Gulf
states should continue to add value to their oil by further developing their petrochemical industries. Oil and gas, however, are not
the region's only potential sources of energy. "Green" energy, particularly in the form of solar power and wind, also holds great development potential. A number of Arab governments have started
to make ambitious plans to develop renewable energy – Morocco,
for example, hopes to have renewable energy provide 40 per cent
of its power needs by 2020, while Egypt and Jordan have targets of
20 per cent and 10 per cent, respectively, by that date. Many North
African countries are also well suited to export captured solar and
renewable energy across the Mediterranean to Europe. Meanwhile,
the UAE, Saudi Arabia, and Kuwait have initiated large-scale renewable energy development plants. By far the most impressive is
the UAE's Masdar City, a mix of residential, business, and commercial buildings that operate on solar energy, with pedestrian and
bike-friendly transportation throughout. Importantly, as this promising energy sector expands, it will provide jobs for Arab engineers, technicians, electricians, project managers, and geologists.

Telecommunications is another key industry in the Arab region,
both financially and in terms of job creation. Telecom infrastructure is now approaching maturity in much of the Arab world, and
mobile penetration is near saturation, which will open a new frontier for mobile-based business.[20] Indeed, there is already a strong
demand for superb service and products from the mobile sector.
With the rapid rise of smartphone technology, there are great possibilities to leverage this into mobile banking, improved content
development, improved user interface, and e-commerce. Granted,
the Arab region has yet to take off in terms of payment and banking by smartphone, but, following the trajectory of other markets,
this is expected to slowly gain traction as confidence in online security increases.

According to the United Nations Economic and Social Commission for Western Asia, there is also high demand in the region for
digital content in Arabic – in communications, news, media and

entertainment, e-books, e-commerce, and so on – and as more Arabs go online, thousands of jobs will be created to fill this as-yet untapped market.[21] One of the most interesting developments is the boost this demand for digital content has given to e-learning, specifically Massive Open Online Courses (MOOCs) that offer free, Internet-based learning to anyone with online access. Startup MOOC type companies such as Nefham, Edraak, Tahrir Academy, and SkillAcademy are slowly filling the need to bring critical thinking skills to Arab youth with formal education. Jordan, for example, is now exporting Arabic digital content across the region, including unique educational interfaces, animation series, and specialized software. In 2011, Jordan employed more than eleven thousand people in this nascent US$500 million industry, a number that is projected to grow to thirty-five thousand as more users go mobile.[22] Internet-savvy Arab youth thus are poised to benefit from the types of jobs this sector offers, including sales, web design, marketing, journalism, software development, and content development.

Finally, the significance of the hospitality and tourism sector in the Arab region cannot be overlooked, given the diversity of its historical, cultural, and natural landscapes. As the non-Western world grows wealthier, tourism could benefit from new travellers to the region. Investment in hospitality and tourism has proved to be a rewarding strategy for economic development and diversification.[23] Medical tourism is also a growing niche that could be further expanded to court visitors – Jordan and the UAE have already started to attract regional and international attention for their state-of-the-art health care services. In addition to infusing local economies with hard currency and supporting infrastructure development, the hospitality and tourism sectors provide important employment opportunities for people as guides, curators, translators, and artists, for example, as well as in education, conservation, marketing, and more.

Thanks to renewed investment by a number of Gulf carriers, Arab airlines have emerged as serious competitors on the world stage. For example, when it commenced operations in the mid-1980s, Dubai's Emirates Airlines carried 255,000 passengers; in 2014 it carried nearly 24 million passengers. The airline sector is expected to experience steady growth in the coming years as new routes and carriers emerge. Indeed, in my own travels to the UAE's impressive airports, it is clear that the Emirates have become a sought-after hub for travellers from across the globe. Construction and development of the Arab region's airports are evident, with Dubai International Airport, for example, soon able to boast the capacity to transit 100 million or more travellers every year, while nearby Al Maktoum International Airport will have an even higher capacity of 160–210 million travellers by 2030.[24] This is most impressive growth, particularly given that successful Arab airlines help to improve the global image of the region, as well as bringing travellers closer to its people and societies.

The Political Imperative for Job Creation

Arab youth today have an entrepreneurial, progressive, and more cosmopolitan spirit that sets them apart from their parents' generation. Although this might not be surprising to those who study the world's youth, when it comes to the Arab region there is an implicit assumption that things are getting worse. I hope I have gone some way to dispelling that misconception, but I do not mean to explain away or excuse the shortcomings of Arab governments or to sugar-coat the challenges Arab countries face. On the contrary, one of my main objectives has been to encourage regional and international policy-makers to take advantage of the demographic dividend that Arab youth represent.

The Arab Spring was a rude awakening for government leaders who thought the status quo was enough to ensure complacency in Arab societies. Despite some promises of democratic change, growing civil debates, and increased activism throughout the region, there has been far too much regression in countries such as Egypt, Libya, Yemen, Iraq, and, of course, Syria. But just as Arab governments were not stable in 2010, they remain vulnerable to further protest and demonstrations for substantive change. Arab youth will continue to drive economic, political, and social transformation in their societies.

As Arab youth take more leadership roles in their political systems, the diplomatic relationship between the West and the Arab world will also need to change. For far too long, there has been a marriage of convenience between Western governments and Arab autocrats such as Libya's Gaddafi and Egypt's Mubarak for oil or valuable geostrategic positions, much to the dismay of many Arabs. The Arab youth I have introduced to you in this book are examples of the potential for the Arab world's rising productive capacity. With the right investments, there is immense opportunity for economic prosperity and growth throughout the region, given its educated and eager workforce. The challenge will be to ensure that Western firms do not appear complicit in the political trappings and inefficiencies of Arab bureaucracies, or guilty of currying favour with the region's crony capitalists. Western businesses must operate in an open investment environment and duly report their dealings with Arab governments. Above all, both sides must do business in a transparent, accountable, and responsible political way. Western businesses should not forget that the Arab masses are watching their own governments, and as the wave of democratization returns to the region, they will reprimand companies and foreign governments that deal with corrupt regimes. Western businesses that increase investment in the Arab world must do so by meeting the needs of the Arab people. If they do, they will bring positive returns – financial, political, and diplomatic – to the Arab region.

Sectarianism, Violence, and Arab Youth

Throughout this book, I have tried to highlight the stories and perspectives – the desires, hopes, and dreams – of young Arabs. Of course, they are also greatly concerned about the rise of violence, sectarianism, and civil war in the Arab world. To be sure, many of the changes Arab youth want to see are complicated by the region's geopolitical challenges, and in speaking to Arab youth, I found that many also recognize that Arab governments frequently use these challenges to forestall the reforms needed for a better future.

Perhaps the issue most gripping the headlines today is of sectarian tensions between Sunni and Shiite Muslims and between Coptic Christians and Sunni Muslims, and the many difficult challenges religious minorities of all kinds face in the Arab region. Violence and civil wars have captured global attention, especially with the rise of new terrorist groups such as ISIS. I do not mean to diminish the real challenges these conflicts pose, but I do want to emphasize that this violence is *not* actually region-wide.

Lebanon, Syria, and Iraq are undoubtedly the most vulnerable to sectarianism of the eighteen countries of North Africa and the Middle East that this book covers. These three are the most ethnically and religiously diverse in the Arab region. The spillover of Syria's revolution-turned-civil-war into Lebanon and Iraq is as unfortunate as it is real: sectarianism and intercommunal violence are strong in these countries, and in no way do I wish to minimize the effect of these factors on this generation of youth.

I asked a twenty-one-year-old Syrian, Melhem, what he thought of the rise of sectarianism in his country. He pointedly replied: "It's like we are watching a soccer match that never use[d] to be on TV and we are now asked to pick a team to support. Five years ago, I had no 'team' to rally behind and I'm hopeful that, in five years' time, we won't be concerned with this awful game." The Arab region is in geopolitical flux, and although sectarianism might have inflicted deep wounds in some countries, let us not assume that these wounds will never heal – Melhem, after all, is hopeful. And as a measure of hope, Amaney Jamal of Princeton University and Michael Hoffman of Georgetown University recently used polling data to confirm that the vast majority of Arabs, including in volatile places such as Egypt and Iraq, are tolerant of Christians and other religious minorities in their countries.[25] The rise of extremism, violence, and terrorism in Libya, Iraq, Egypt, Syria, Lebanon, and elsewhere is disheartening, but one should take comfort in the knowledge that the vast majority of Arabs have negative views of movements such as ISIS, al-Qaeda, Hezbollah, and Hamas. In fact, concerns about extremism are unprecedentedly high throughout the region, and as many terrorist attacks hit closer and closer to home, the societal uproar rises against those movements and groups who use violence to achieve political aims.[26] A March 2015 survey conducted by the Palestinian Center for Policy and Survey Research found that an "overwhelming majority of 86% [of respondents] believes that ISIS is a radical group that does not represent true Islam."[27] A majority of Arabs polled also support the international airstrikes against ISIS, although they have notable concerns about the collateral killing of innocent civilians and legitimate fears about mission creep.[28]

In countries that are not ravaged by sectarianism, there is an apparent disbelief among many Arab youths that this is even happening in their region. Travelling there, one hears the opinion that all of the violence is foreign directed. It is, indeed, a pervasive view that sectarianism and the rise of ISIS are somehow a Western project designed to ruin the region. As an academic, my initial reaction to this line of thought was to judge it as stemming simply from ignorance, until I began to see it more as a coping mechanism in the face of an awful reality. Countless times I have heard statements such as, "Islam doesn't support violence against minorities, so this can't be committed by Muslims," or "We never had sectarianism until the US invaded Iraq," or "ISIS came from nowhere. It is not Muslims who are fighting in ISIS." None of these is true, of course, but I cannot help but think that any reasonable person would prefer these explanations, no matter how untrue, rather than acknowledge that communal violence, sectarianism, and terrorism have in some way informed or infiltrated Arab values. It gives me hope that so many Arabs openly and adamantly reject extremism as a cultural and social value. Nevertheless, there is an enormous need to heal wounds created by sectarianism and violence, just as there is a need for the Arab region to undertake some soul searching and to understand why and how the region came to the place it is today.

The onus of soul searching here is primarily on Arab governments. They absolutely must not play the sectarian card, and must stop leaving their failings on the doorsteps of foreign governments when domestic failures are clearly complicit. And they must explain why and how they plan to take part in the fight against terrorist groups. The lack of transparency in the Arab region has only furthered societal misunderstandings, conspiracy theories, and poor media standards of reporting. In the fight against ISIS and al-Qaeda – two groups that have terrorized and killed many more Muslims than non-Muslims – Arab governments should not equate organizations of this kind with broader non-violent Islamist political movements. Arab governments – such as those of Tunisia, Morocco, and, albeit intermittently, Jordan – that have been able to find a space for such movements have prospered to some extent, both politically and economically. The temptation to paint Islamists with a broad brush is sure to backfire politically on Arab governments. Younger Arabs might be less dogmatic about their faith, but they are still generally spiritual believers, and a struggle against non-violent Islamists would only further alienate this generation.

Finally, it continues to give me hope that, in a city like Baghdad, seemingly at the heart of sectarian conflict in Iraq, more than 30 per cent of the population has both a Shiite and a Sunni parent. At the height of the sectarian battles in the Iraqi government in mid-2014, an online Twitter campaign of individuals who identified as both Sunni and Shiite used the hashtag #Sushi to identify themselves and reach out to one another. The "Sushi" movement reminds me that the future of Arab youth will be determined by economic and political opportunities, rather than by anachronistic religious divisions. Arab youth are frustrated with the broken nature of their social systems, which fixate on divisions and differences. To see them one day in positions of leadership and political power will be a cause for celebration.

To stem the rise of violence, Arab governments must give their people – their youth, in particular – a cause for hope and optimism by creating good jobs and providing the socio-economic and political conditions that allow people to flourish and have a stake in a stable, prosperous society. Sectarianism arises in countries with poor governance, where political systems benefit parties that focus on divisions instead of on commonalities. Political parties must move their discourse away from the narrow platform of ethnic and religious identity. This has yet to happen in Iraq and Lebanon, where deep sectarian identities remain. Political leaders who play the sectarian card are merely fuelling the fire of sectarianism. This needs to stop. Arab youth deserve a better future, and governments need to work harder to deliver that future.

Final Thoughts

I hope the reader will agree that the Arab region is on the cusp of significant change. Whether that change is for the better or worse is a point of considerable debate. In this book I have tried to show that Arab youth are different than previous generations and a source of great hope. In his book *The New Arabs*, Juan Cole takes readers deeper into revolutionary world history to argue that youth will push the Arab region to a better political future.[29] Marwan Muasher, in *The Second Arab Awakening*, suggests that the Arab Spring was a cry for pluralism and tolerance on which Arab youth have not yet given up.[30] Like Cole and Muasher, I believe that the Arab Spring was just the beginning, and that one needs to take a longer historical view to see the fruit of these revolutions to overthrow stagnant autocrats. The challenges that Arab youth face are considerable, but there are many reasons to be optimistic about the generation that will lead the region in the coming decades. Too many clichéd views of the Arab world do not match its reality. True, parts of the region are underdeveloped, political propaganda brings to mind Orwell's *Animal Farm*, and many people maintain old and unyielding religious views. But this does not represent the Arab world as a whole. Youth increasingly mock, criticize, and reject forces that prevent them from excelling in a modern world they yearn to join. I have faith that the majority of Arab youth will prevail against these forces, and I hope that, having read this book, you will share this sense of optimism.

Appendix

Chapter One

Table 1: Real Growth of Gross Domestic Product, Arab Countries, 1993–2013

Country	1993–98	1998–2003	2003–08	2008–13
	(% change over 5-year period)			
Algeria	13.8	24.9	18.5	14.8
Bahrain	16.6	23.7	39.9	19.2
Egypt	25.4	22.3	33.3	16.9
Iraq	–	–	91.6	40.8
Jordan	21.1	25.0	47.2	16.9
Kuwait	21.5	25.2	42.4	–
Lebanon	22.5	11.9	33.9	25.3
Libya	–	–	33.7	−24.7
Morocco	21.8	20.7	26.1	22.2
Oman	22.3	16.4	36.7	23.1
Palestinian territories	–	8.2	0.1	–
Qatar	–	–	124.5	62.4
Saudi Arabia	10.0	13.5	41.4	30.5
Sudan	30.8	33.9	41.2	−12.7
Syria	28.7	11.1	–	–
Tunisia	25.0	24.0	28.9	14.6
United Arab Emirates	30.9	28.9	34.4	–
Yemen	31.6	23.3	21.7	−2.5

Source: World Bank, *World Development Indicators* (Washington, DC, 2014); available online at http://databank.worldbank.org/data/reports.aspx?source=world-development-indicators.

Table 2: Dependency Ratio, Arab Countries, 1998–2013

Country	1998	2003	2008	2013
	(% to working age)			
Algeria	67.6	53.6	47.1	47.9
Bahrain	49.9	46.5	31.1	30.3
Egypt	71.7	63.8	59.3	58.5
Iraq	88.1	84.2	82.0	76.2
Jordan	74.6	71.9	65.3	60.2
Kuwait	39.5	40.9	38.7	37.2
Lebanon	57.2	55.5	51.1	41.8
Libya	63.3	55.3	51.9	52.1
Morocco	66.9	58.6	51.5	48.9
Oman	67.6	63.4	50.3	35.7
Palestinian territories	100.3	96.8	86.2	75.6
Qatar	37.8	39.7	20.9	17.2
Saudi Arabia	75.4	64.5	54.0	46.9
Sudan	88.5	86.8	84.1	79.9
Syria	82.4	75.3	67.4	64.3
Tunisia	59.7	50.9	44.9	43.6
United Arab Emirates	37.1	32.3	18.1	18.6
Yemen	110.5	98.7	85.4	75.6

Note: Dependants include all residents ages 0–14 and 65+; "working age" people are ages 15–64. The ratio is determined by the following equation:

$$100\% \times \frac{(People\ 0-14 + People\ 65+)}{People\ 15-64}$$

Source: World Bank, *World Development Indicators* (Washington, DC, 2014); available online at http://databank.worldbank.org/data/reports.aspx?source=world-development-indicators.

Chapter Two

Table 3: Net Foreign Direct Investment Inflows, Arab Countries, 1998–2013

Country	1998	2003	2008	2013
	(% of gross domestic product)			
Algeria	1.3	0.9	1.5	0.8
Bahrain	2.9	4.7	7.0	3.0
Egypt	1.3	0.3	5.8	2.0
Iraq	–	–	1.4	1.3
Jordan	3.9	5.4	12.9	5.3
Kuwait	0.2	−0.1	0.0	–
Lebanon	–	14.2	15.0	6.4
Libya	−0.5	0.6	4.4	0.9
Morocco	0.0	4.6	2.8	3.2
Oman	0.7	0.1	4.9	2.0
Palestinian territories	5.5	0.5	0.8	–
Qatar	3.4	2.7	3.3	−0.4
Saudi Arabia	2.9	−0.3	7.6	1.2
Sudan	3.3	7.6	3.1	3.3
Syria	0.5	0.7	–	–
Tunisia	3.0	2.0	5.8	2.3
United Arab Emirates	0.3	3.4	4.4	–
Yemen	−3.5	−0.8	5.1	−0.4

Source: World Bank, *World Development Indicators* (Washington, DC, 2014); available online at http://databank.worldbank.org/data/reports.aspx?source=world-development-indicators.

Table 4: Mobile Phone Subscriptions, Arab Countries, 1998–2013

Country	1998	2003	2008	2013
	(per 100,000 people)			
Algeria	58	4,384	75,665	102,011
Bahrain	14,908	57,393	129,098	165,909
Egypt	142	8,350	54,690	121,508
Iraq	0	308	59,562	96,105
Jordan	1,780	26,594	89,890	141,796
Kuwait	14,516	67,097	55,507	190,288
Lebanon	16,227	21,557	34,089	80,564
Libya	399	2,342	125,563	165,045
Morocco	416	24,875	73,706	128,525
Oman	4,514	24,863	124,130	154,646
Palestinian territories	–	7,707	34,431	73,741
Qatar	11,948	57,030	105,178	152,644
Saudi Arabia	3,253	31,674	136,538	176,498
Sudan	26	1,439	28,954	72,852
Syria	0	6,850	34,681	55,975
Tunisia	417	19,473	82,781	115,604
United Arab Emirates	17,915	88,219	137,641	171,874
Yemen	97	3,538	29,696	69,015

Source: World Bank, *World Development Indicators* (Washington, DC, 2014); available online at http://databank.worldbank.org/data/reports.aspx?source=world-development-indicators.

Table 5: Youth Enrolment in Postsecondary Education, Arab Countries, 1998–2013

Country	1998	2003	2008	2013
		(% enrolled)		
Algeria	–	16.7	22.3	31.5
Bahrain	–	–	–	33.5
Egypt	–	32.3	31.9	30.1
Iraq	–	12.7	–	–
Jordan	23.4	30.8	41.2	46.6
Kuwait	22.6	23.8	–	–
Lebanon	–	44.9	46.7	46.3
Libya	–	59.2	–	–
Morocco	11.7	10.2	11.8	–
Oman	6.7	15.0	21.1	–
Palestinian territories	19.0	28.0	48.9	49.1
Qatar	26.5	16.4	13.3	12.1
Saudi Arabia	18.0	23.4	29.7	50.9
Sudan	–	–	–	–
Syria	–	12.4	22.6	–
Tunisia	13.9	22.7	31.1	35.2
United Arab Emirates	–	–	–	–
Yemen	4.9	10.6	10.5	–

Source: World Bank, *World Development Indicators* (Washington, DC, 2014); available online at http://databank.worldbank.org/data/reports.aspx?source=world-development-indicators.

Table 6: Urban Population, Arab Countries, 1998–2013

Country	1998	2003	2008	2013
	(% urban)			
Algeria	58.3	62.3	66.1	69.5
Bahrain	88.4	88.4	88.5	88.7
Egypt	42.7	42.9	43.1	43.0
Iraq	68.4	68.7	68.9	69.3
Jordan	79.2	80.6	82.0	83.2
Kuwait	98.1	98.2	98.2	98.3
Lebanon	85.8	86.3	86.9	87.5
Libya	76.2	76.7	77.3	78.2
Morocco	52.7	54.3	56.7	59.2
Oman	71.6	71.5	74.1	76.7
Palestinian territories	71.5	72.6	73.7	74.8
Qatar	95.9	96.9	98.3	99.1
Saudi Arabia	79.4	80.5	81.6	82.7
Sudan	32.4	32.7	32.9	33.5
Syria	51.2	53.0	54.9	56.9
Tunisia	62.7	64.6	65.6	66.5
United Arab Emirates	79.4	81.5	83.4	85.0
Yemen	25.2	27.8	30.6	33.5

Source: World Bank, *World Development Indicators* (Washington, DC, 2014); available online at http://databank.worldbank.org/data/reports.aspx?source=world-development-indicators.

Chapter Three

Table 7: Democratization Score, Arab Countries, 1998–2013

Country	1998	2003	2008	2013
Algeria	−3	−3	2	2
Bahrain	−9	−7	−7	−10
Egypt	−6	−6	−3	−4
Iraq	−9	−	−	3
Jordan	−2	−2	−3	−3
Kuwait	−7	−7	−7	−7
Lebanon	−	−	6	6
Libya	−7	−7	−7	−
Morocco	−6	−6	−6	−4
Oman	−9	−8	−8	−8
Palestinian territories	−	−	−	−
Qatar	−10	−10	−10	−10
Saudi Arabia	−10	−10	−10	−10
Sudan	−7	−6	−4	−4
Syria	−9	−7	−7	−9
Tunisia	−3	−4	−4	−
United Arab Emirates	−8	−8	−8	−8
Yemen	−2	−2	−2	3

Note: Scores towards −10 mean more autocratic, with −10 being the most autocratic; scores towards 10 mean more democratic, with 10 being the most democratic.

Source: Center for Systemic Peace, "INSCR Data Page: Polity IV Annual Time-Series, 1800–2013" (Vienna, VA, 2014); available online at http://www.systemicpeace.org/inscrdata.html.

Table 8: Corruption Perceptions Index, Arab Countries, 1998–2013

Country	1998	2003	2008	2013
Algeria	–	26	32	36
Bahrain	–	61	54	48
Egypt	29	33	28	32
Iraq	–	22	13	16
Jordan	47	46	51	45
Kuwait	–	53	43	43
Lebanon	–	30	30	28
Libya	–	21	26	15
Morocco	37	33	35	37
Oman	–	63	55	47
Palestinian territories	–	30	–	–
Qatar	–	56	65	68
Saudi Arabia	–	45	35	46
Sudan	–	23	16	11
Syria	–	34	21	17
Tunisia	50	49	44	41
United Arab Emirates	–	52	59	69
Yemen	–	26	23	18

Note: Scores towards 100 are perceived as less corrupt, with 100 being
the least corrupt.

Source: Transparency International, "Corruption Perceptions Index" (Berlin, 2014);
available online at http://www.transparency.org/research/cpi/overview.

Table 9: Internet Users, Arab Countries, 1998–2013

Country	1998	2003	2008	2013
	(% of population with Internet access)			
Algeria	0.0	2.2	10.2	16.5
Bahrain	3.2	21.6	52.0	90.0
Egypt	0.1	4.0	18.0	49.6
Iraq	–	0.6	1.0	9.2
Jordan	1.3	8.5	23.0	44.2
Kuwait	3.1	22.4	42.0	75.5
Lebanon	2.7	8.0	22.5	70.5
Libya	–	2.8	9.0	16.5
Morocco	0.1	3.4	33.1	56.0
Oman	0.9	7.3	20.0	66.5
Palestinian territories	–	4.1	24.4	46.6
Qatar	3.5	19.2	44.3	85.3
Saudi Arabia	0.1	8.0	36.0	60.5
Sudan	0.0	0.5	–	22.7
Syria	0.1	3.4	14.0	26.2
Tunisia	0.1	6.5	27.5	43.8
United Arab Emirates	6.9	29.5	63.0	88.0
Yemen	0.0	0.6	6.9	20.0

Source: World Bank, *World Development Indicators* (Washington, DC, 2014); available online at http://databank.worldbank.org/data/reports.aspx?source=world-development-indicators.

Table 10: Press Freedom Index, Arab Countries, 2003–13

Country	2003	2008	2013
Algeria	26	32	36
Bahrain	61	54	48
Egypt	33	28	32
Iraq	22	13	16
Jordan	46	51	45
Kuwait	53	43	43
Lebanon	30	30	28
Libya	21	26	15
Morocco	33	35	37
Oman	63	55	47
Palestinian territories	30	–	–
Qatar	56	65	68
Saudi Arabia	45	35	46
Sudan	23	16	11
Syria	34	21	17
Tunisia	49	44	41
United Arab Emirates	52	59	69
Yemen	26	23	18

Note: Scores towards 100 represent a freer press, with 100 being the most free.

Source: Reporters Without Borders, "World Press Freedom Index 2014"; available online at http://en.rsf.org/spip.php?page=classement&id_rubrique=1054.

Chapter Five

Table 11: Arab Migrants Abroad, 2010

Country of Origin	Total	United States & Canada	Europe	Latin America	Africa	Asia	Other Arab Countries
				(millions)			
Algeria	1.21	0.04	1.08	0	0.01	0.05	0.03
Bahrain	0.03	0.01	0.01	0	0	0.01	0.01
Egypt	3.74	0.18	0.22	0	0.01	0.08	3.25
Iraq	1.55	0.14	0.30	0	0	0.55	0.56
Jordan	0.73	0.08	0.03	0	0	0.01	0.61
Kuwait	0.26	0.04	0.01	0	0	0.01	0.20
Lebanon	0.66	0.22	0.18	0.03	0.01	0.10	0.13
Libya	0.11	0.01	0.03	0	0.01	0.03	0.02
Morocco	3.02	0.13	2.59	0	0	0.25	0.05
Oman	0.02	0	0	0	0	0	0.01
Palestinian territories	3.02	0.01	0.01	0	0	0	2.99
Qatar	0.01	0	0	0	0	0	0
Saudi Arabia	0.18	0.05	0.03	0	0	0.02	0.07
Sudan	0.97	0.05	0.04	0	0.31	0.03	0.54
Syria	0.95	0.09	0.11	0.02	0	0.04	0.69
Tunisia	0.65	0.02	0.50	0	0	0.02	0.12
United Arab Emirates	0.06	0.02	0	0	0	0.02	0.02
Yemen	1.13	0.06	0.02	0	0	0.05	1.00

Source: World Bank, "Migration & Remittances Data: Bilateral Migration Matrix 2010" (Washington, DC, 2013); available online at http://econ.worldbank.org/WBSITE/EXTERNAL/EXTDEC/EXTDECPROSPECT S/0,,contentMDK:22759429~pagePK:64165401~piPK:64165026~theSitePK:476883,00.html.

Table 12: Inflows of Remittances to Arab Countries from Top 5 Source Countries and Others, 2012

Receiving Country	Total	Saudi Arabia	France	Jordan	United States	Kuwait	Other
				(US$ millions)			
Algeria	1,843	0	1,399	3	12	0	429
Bahrain	–	–	–	–	–	–	–
Egypt	20,515	5,667	172	3,809	880	2,181	7,806
Iraq	381	0	1	58	33	0	289
Jordan	3,643	948	6	–	470	0	2,219
Kuwait	–	–	–	–	–	–	–
Lebanon	7,472	627	513	152	1,538	0	4,642
Libya	–	–	–	–	–	–	–
Morocco	6,894	43	1,946	8	214	0	4,683
Oman	39	0	0	13	4	0	22
Palestinian territories	–	–	–	–	–	–	–
Qatar	–	–	–	–	–	–	–
Saudi Arabia	245	0	2	55	58	0	130
Sudan	1,126	–	3	20	77	0	1,026
Syria	2,079	255	41	513	185	348	737
Tunisia	2,198	40	1,043	6	31	0	1,078
United Arab Emirates	–	–	–	–	–	–	–
Yemen	1,487	1,142	3	17	99	0	226

Source: World Bank, "Migration & Remittances Data: Bilateral Remittances Matrices" (Washington, DC, 2013); available online at http://econ.worldbank.org/WBSITE/EXTERNAL/EXTDEC/EXTDECPROSPECTS/0,,contentMDK:22759429~pagePK:64165401~piPK:64165026~theSitePK:476883,00.html.

Table 13: Arab Students Enrolled Abroad, Top 5 Destination Countries and Others, 2012

Country of Origin	Total	France	United States	United Arab Emirates	United Kingdom	Jordan	Other
Algeria	24,881	21,804	171	299	183	35	2,389
Bahrain	4,501	34	424	467	1,112	673	1,791
Egypt	16,477	1,177	2,132	2,948	1,156	455	8,609
Iraq	14,739	268	784	2,197	1,251	2,959	7,280
Jordan	17,088	157	1,997	4,313	1,394	–	9,227
Kuwait	11,061	96	3,605	963	1,816	1,722	2,859
Lebanon	13,323	4,567	1,308	1,252	675	170	5,351
Libya	6,738	352	1,286	120	1,755	76	3,149
Morocco	43,814	28,778	1,264	256	337	28	13,151
Oman	10,443	27	521	5,186	1,202	1,079	2,428
Palestinian territories	17,922	191	321	3,816	176	7,337	6,081
Qatar	3,827	53	948	330	1,252	219	1,025
Saudi Arabia	62,852	539	33,066	1,289	9,773	3,295	14,890
Sudan	3,297	59	231	5	5	83	2,914
Syria	18,463	1,828	444	3,525	668	1,990	10,008
Tunisia	19,109	11,134	431	114	79	44	7,307
United Arab Emirates	8,887	248	2,031	–	3,089	58	3,461
Yemen	15,293	112	261	2,148	129	843	11,800

Source: UNESCO, "Global Flow of Tertiary-Level Students" (Paris, 2014); available online from http://www.uis.unesco.org/Education/Pages/international-student-flow-viz.aspx.

Conclusion

Table 14: Total Job Recruitment Ads Placed in the Arab World, by Country, 2014

Country	Total Job Recruitment Ads	% of Total
United Arab Emirates	2,765	56
Qatar	896	18
Saudi Arabia	741	15
Kuwait	198	4
Oman	153	3
Egypt	72	1
Bahrain	62	1
Iraq	51	1
Other*	42	1
Total	4,976	100

* Consists of Lebanon, Jordan, Morocco, Sudan, Tunisia, Libya, Algeria, and Yemen.

Source: GulfTalent, "Recruitment & Jobs in the Middle East" (30 October 2014); available online at http://www.gulftalent.com/jobs.

Table 15: Economic Growth by Sector, United Arab Emirates, 2000–12

Sector	Growth, 2000–12	Average Annual Growth
	(% change)	
Mining and quarrying	112.82	8.68
Crude oil and natural gas	113.31	8.72
Manufacturing industries	−10.85	−0.83
Electricity, gas, and water	81.26	6.25
Construction	23.44	1.80
Wholesale and retail trade and repairing services	−21.36	−1.64
Restaurants and hotels	4.79	0.37
Transport, storage, and communication	37.87	2.91
Real estate and business services	15.14	1.16
Social and personal services	49.37	3.80
Financial corporations	53.65	4.13

Source: United Arab Emirates, Bureau of Statistics, "Statistics by Subject: National Accounts" (2014); available online at http://www.uaestatistics.gov.ae/ ReportsByDepartmentEnglish/tabid/104/Default.aspx?MenuId=1 .UAEBureauofStatistics(2014).

Table 16: Distribution of Job Ad Postings by Job Category, Middle East, 2014

Job Category	Number of Positions	% of Total Positions
Civil engineering	1,153	23.2
Finance and construction	265	5.3
Sales	264	5.3
Human resources	262	5.3
Retail sales	260	5.2
Administration	257	5.2
Management	250	5.0
Accounting	240	4.8
Marketing	227	4.6
Mechanical engineering	171	3.4
Software	163	3.3
Legal	145	2.9
Logistics	135	2.7
Network administration	129	2.6
Petroleum engineering	117	2.4
Customer service	112	2.3
Electronics engineering	101	2.0
All others	725	14.6
Total	4,976	100.0

Source: GulfTalent, "Recruitment & Jobs in the Middle East" (30 October 2014); available online at http://www.gulftalent.com/jobs.

Notes

1 Introduction

1 Samuel P. Huntington, *The Clash of Civilizations and the Remaking of World Order* (New York: Simon & Schuster, 1994), 119.
2 Richard Florida, "The Revolt of the Creative Class," *Atlantic*, 3 March 2011; available online at http://www.theatlantic.com/international/archive/2011/03/the-revolt-of-the-creative-class/71829/.
3 OECD-MENA Investment Programme, "Gender Inequality and Entrepreneurship in the Middle East and North Africa: A Statistical Portrait" (paper prepared for the OECD-MENA Women's Business Forum annual meeting, Rabat, Morocco, 2 December 2013); available online at http://www.oecd.org/mena/investment/Statistical%20Portrait.pdf.
4 Bassem Aoun, "Entrepreneurship for growth," *Your Middle East*, 23 August 2013; available online at http://www.yourmiddleeast.com/business/entrepreneurship-for-growth-starting-small-not-a-bad-idea_17312.
5 United Nations Human Settlements Programme, "The State of Arab Cities 2012: Challenges of Urban Transition" (Nairobi, Kenya: UN-Habitat, 2012), viii.
6 United Nations Educational, Scientific and Cultural Organization (UNESCO), "A Generation on the Move: Insights into the Conditions, Aspirations, and Activism of Arab youth" (Beirut: Isaam Fares Institute for Public Policy and International Affairs, November 2011), 25.
7 See Kate Seelye, "After the Arab Spring, Arab art blossoms," *Middle East Institute*, 31 March 2014; available online at http://www.mei.edu/content/after-spring-arab-art-blossoms.

2 Bread

1 World Bank, "World Development Indicators, General Government Final Consumption as a percentage of GDP" (Washington, DC, 2014); available online at http://data.worldbank.org/indicator/NE.CON .GOVT.ZS. In developing countries, public spending decreased from 17.6 per cent in the 1980s to 15.3 per cent in the 1990s and to 14.4 per cent in the 2000s.
2 See Janine Clark, *Islam, Charity, and Activism: Middle-Class Networks and Social Welfare in Egypt, Jordan, and Yemen* (Bloomington: Indiana University Press, 2004).
3 Jillian Schwedler, "Amman Cosmopolitan: Spaces and Practices of Aspiration and Consumption," *Comparative Studies of South Asia, Africa and the Middle East* 30, no. 3 (2010): 947–62.
4 CBS News, "How a Slap Sparked Tunisia's Revolution," *60 Minutes*, 22 February 2011; available online at http://www.cbsnews.com/news/ how-a-slap-sparked-tunisias-revolution-22-02-2011/.
5 Vincent Romani, "The Politics of Higher Education in the Middle East: Problems and Prospects," *Middle East Brief*, May 2009, 1.
6 UNESCO, "A Decade of Higher Education in the Arab States: Achievements and Challenges," Regional Report (Beirut: UNESCO Regional Bureau for Education in the Arab States, July 2009), 11.
7 Ibid.
8 Shiekha Abdulla Al-Misnad, "The Dearth of Qatari Men in Higher Education" (Washington, DC: Middle East Institute, June 2012); available online at http://www.mei.edu/content/dearth-qatari-men-higher-education-reasons-and-implications.
9 United Arab Emirates, Ministry of Education, "Annual Report on Schools in the Emirate of Ras Al Khaimah, Ministry of Education, Ras Al Khaimah" (Ras Al Khaimah, UAE: Sheikh Saud bin Saqr Al Qasimi Foundation, 2008); UNESCO, "Education for All by 2015: Will We Make It?" Education for All Global Monitoring Report (Oxford: Oxford University Press, 2008).
10 Fatma Abdulla, "Emirati Women: Conceptions of Education and Employment," in *Soaring Beyond Boundaries: Women Breaking Educational Barriers in Traditional Societies*, ed. R.O Mabokela, 73–112 (Netherlands: Sense, 2007).
11 World Bank, "Free to Prosper, Jobs in the Middle East and North Africa" (Washington DC, 2013), 2.

12 "Growing number of Saudi single women challenge tradition," *Saudi Gazette*, 21 January 2014; available online at http://www.saudigazette.com.sa/index.cfm?method=home.regcon&contentid=20150122231244.

13 Louise Redvers, "Keys to the Kingdom: The Slow Rise of Saudi Women," *BBC Online*, 9 April 2015; available online at http://www.bbc.com/capital/story/20150408-slow-gains-for-saudi-women.

14 Times Higher Education, "The BRICS & Emerging Economies Rankings 2014"; available online at https://www.timeshighereducation.co.uk/world-university-rankings/2014/brics-and-emerging-economies#/.

15 Bessma Momani and Wafaa Hasan, "Arab Scholar's Take on Globalization," in *Thinking International Relations Differently*, ed. Arlene B. Tickner and David L. Blaney, 228–50 (London: Routledge, 2012).

16 Arab American Institute, "Attitudes of Arabs (2005)" (Washington, DC, 2012); available online at http://www.aaiusa.org/attitudes-of-arabs-2005.

17 Melani Cammett and Ishac Diwan, *The Political Economy of the Arab Uprisings* (Boulder, CO: Westview Press, 2013).

18 Mark Dabrowski, "Macroeconomic and Fiscal Challenges Faced by the Southern and Eastern Mediterranean Region," CASE Research Paper 471/2014 (Warsaw: Center for Social and Economic Research, February 2014).

19 International Monetary Fund (IMF), *Gulf Cooperation Council Countries: Enhancing Economic Outcomes in an Uncertain Global Economy* (Washington, DC, 2011); available online at https://www.imf.org/external/pubs/ft/dp/2011/1101mcd.pdf.

20 United Nations Development Programme (UNDP), *Arab Development Challenges Report, 2011: Towards the Developmental State in the Arab Region* (Cairo: UNDP, Regional Centre for Arab States, 2011), 17–18.

21 Marcus Noland and Howard Pack, *The Arab Economies in a Changing World* (Washington, DC: Peterson Institute for International Economics, 2011), 66.

22 Cammett and Diwan, *Political Economy of the Arab Uprisings*, 21.

23 IMF, "Economic Transformation in MENA: Delivering on the Promise of Shared Prosperity" (Washington, DC, 27 May 2011); available online at http://www.imf.org/external/np/g8/pdf/052711.pdf.

24 Magdi Amin et al., *After the Spring: Economic Transitions in the Arab World* (New York: Oxford University Press, 2012), 55.

25 Ted R. Gurr, *Why Men Rebel* (Princeton, NJ: Princeton University Press, 1970), 23.

26 World Bank, "Free to Prosper," 3.

27 International Finance Corporation and Islamic Development Bank, *Education for Employment: Realizing Arab Youth Potential* (Washington, DC: World Bank, April 2011); available online at https://www.e4earabyouth .com/pdf/MGLPDF136022536640.pdf.

28 Hala Hattab, "GEM Egypt Report 2012" (London: Global Entrepreneurship Monitor, December 2012), viii, ix.

29 ASDA'A Burson-Marsteller, "Arab Youth Survey 2014" (Dubai, UAE: ASDA'A Burson-Marsteller, 2014), 17; available online at http://www .arabyouthsurvey.com/.

30 Jacqui Kew et al., *Generation Entrepreneur? The State of Global Youth Entrepreneurship* (Washington, DC; London: Global Entrepreneurship Monitor and Youth Business International, September 2013), 66–7. Arab countries surveyed included Algeria, Egypt, the Palestinian territories, and Tunisia. Iran and Israel were omitted from the Middle East category. Developing regions included Latin America and the Caribbean, sub-Saharan Africa, and Asia Pacific and South Asia.

31 Ibid., 64–5.

32 Fadi Salem and Racha Mourtada, "Social Media, Employment and Entrepreneurship," Dubai School of Government Report (Dubai World Trade Centre, UAE: Dubai School of Government/SAP MENA, October 2012), 17.

33 See "Starts of Science" (advertising supplement), *International New York Times*, 4 November 2014, 15.

34 World Bank, "Free to Prosper," Executive Summary, 1.

35 ASDA'A Burson-Marsteller, "Arab Youth Survey 2014," 17.

36 Gabriella Cacciotti and James C. Hayton, "Fear of Failure and Entrepreneurship: A Review and Direction for Future Research," ERC Research Paper 24 (Warwick, UK: Enterprise Research Centre, August 2014), 24.

37 "Tahrir Academy: Empowering self-education through video on YouTube," *Daily News Egypt*, 18 February 2014; available online at http:// www.dailynewsegypt.com/2014/02/18/tahrir-academy-empowering-self-education-video-youtube/.

38 Mariana Mazzucato, *The Entrepreneurial State: Debunking Public vs. Private Sector Myths* (New York: Anthem Press, 2014).

39 Vijay Mahajan, *The Arab World Unbound: Tapping into the Power of 350 Million Consumers* (San Francisco: Jossey-Bass, 2012), 21.

40 Unearthed: Trail of Ibn Battuta Homepage"; available online at http:// unearthedgame.com/.

41 Daniel Johnston, "Shaheen revealed for Tekken 7 as game's first non-stereotypical character," *Independent*, 2 January 2015; available online at http://www.independent.co.uk/life-style/gadgets-and-tech/gaming/tekken-reveals-new-saudi-arabian-character-9953837.html. As of the date of publication of this book, *Tekken 7* has seen limited release in Japan, with a wide release date yet to be announced.

42 Richard Florida, *The Rise of the Creative Class: And How It's Transforming Work, Leisure, Community and Everyday Life* (New York: Basic Books, 2002).

43 UNESCO, "Decade of Higher Education in the Arab States," 45.

44 Ibid.

45 Jamie Peck, "Struggling with the Creative Class," *International Journal of Urban and Regional Research* 29, no. 4 (2005): 740–70.

46 ASDA'A Burson-Marsteller, "Arab Youth Survey 2014," 19.

3 Freedom

 1 See, for example, Eva Bellin, "The Robustness of Authoritarianism in the Middle East: Exceptionalism in Comparative Perspective," *Comparative Politics* 36, no. 2 (2004): 139–57; Jason Brownlee, *Authoritarianism in an Age of Democratization* (Cambridge: Cambridge University Press, 2007); Daniel Brumberg, "Democratization in the Arab World? The Trap of Liberalized Autocracy," *Journal of Democracy* 13, no. 4 (2002): 56–68; Larry Diamond, "Why Are There No Arab Democracies?" *Journal of Democracy* 21, no. 1 (2010): 93–104; Noureddine Jebnoun, Mehrdad Kia, and Mimi Kirk, eds., *Modern Middle East Authoritarianism: Roots, Ramifications, and Crisis* (New York: Routledge, 2013); May Kassem, *In the Guise of Democracy: Governance in Contemporary Egypt* (Reading, UK: Ithaca Press, 1999); Marsha Pripstein-Posusney and Michele Penner Angrist, eds., *Authoritarianism in the Middle East: Regimes and Resistance* (Boulder, CO: Lynne Rienner, 2005); Nicola Pratt, *Democracy and Authoritarianism in the Arab World* (Boulder, CO: Lynne Rienner, 2007); Quintan Wiktorowicz, "The Limits of Democracy in the Middle East: The Case of Jordan," *Middle East Journal* 53, no. 4 (1999): 606–20.

 2 Rex Brynen et al., *Beyond the Arab Spring: Authoritarianism and Democratization in the Arab World* (Boulder, CO: Lynne Rienner, 2012).

 3 Kanan Makiya, *Republic of Fear: The Politics of Modern Iraq* (Berkeley: University of California Press, 1998).

 4 See, for example, Parag Khanna, "The end of the nation-state?" *New York Times*, 12 October 2013; David W. Lesch, "Will Syria war mean end of

Sykes-Picot?" *Al-Monitor*, 12 August 2013, available online at http://
www.al-monitor.com/pulse/originals/2013/08/syria-sykes-picot-
ottoman-borders-breakup-levant-mandates.html; Itamar Rabinovich,
"The End of Sykes-Picot? Reflections on the Prospects of the Arab State
System," Middle East Memo 32 (Washington, DC: Brookings Institution,
2014); Joel Rayburn, "The Coming War in the Middle East," *Defining
Ideas*, 6 February 2013, available online at http://www.hoover.org/
research/coming-war-middle-east; Robin Wright, "Imagining a
remapped Middle East," *New York Times*, 28 September 2013, available
online at http://www.nytimes.com/2013/09/29/opinion/sunday/
imagining-a-remapped-middle-east.html?pagewanted=all.
 5 Arab Advisors Group, "A majority of FTA satellite channels catering to
the Arab World are privately owned," 19 August 2013; available online
at http://www.arabadvisors.com/Pressers/presser-190813.htm.
 6 Richard Shediac, Samer Bohsali, and Hatem Samman, "The Bedrock of
Society: Understanding and Growing the MENA Region's Middle Class,"
Ideation Center Insight Paper (Abu Dhabi, UAE: Booz, 2012), 30.
 7 Karim Sabbagh et al., "Understanding the Arab Digital Generation,"
Ideation Center Insight Paper (Abu Dhabi, UAE: Booz, 2012), 11.
 8 Ibid.
 9 See also Joe F. Khalil, "Youth-Generated Media," in *New Directions in
Middle East and Northern African Studies*, ed. Brian T. Edwards, 47–53
(Doha, Qatar: Northwestern University in Qatar, 2014).
10 Deloitte, "Arab States Mobile Observatory 2013" (London: Groupe
Speciale Mobile Association, 2013), 20.
11 Howard Rheingold, *Smart Mobs: The Next Social Revolution* (New York:
Basic Books, 2007).
12 Go-Gulf, "Smartphone Usage in the Middle East," 2 October 2013;
available online at http://www.go-gulf.ae/blog/smartphone-middle-
east/.
13 Christopher Schroeder, *Startup Rising: The Entrepreneurial Revolution
Remaking the Middle East* (New York: Palgrave Macmillan, 2013), 10–11.
14 Sabbagh et al., "Understanding the Arab Digital Generation," 2. These
nine countries are Saudi Arabia, the UAE, Egypt, Bahrain, Kuwait, Qatar,
Jordan, Algeria, and Lebanon.
15 Ibid., 7.
16 Ibid., 4.
17 Go-Gulf, "Internet Usage in the Middle East," 2 August 2013; available
online at http://www.go-gulf.ae/blog/internet-usage-middle-east/.
18 Sabbagh et al., "Understanding the Arab Digital Generation," 9.

19 Heather Jimaa, "Facebook more popular than YouTube – report," *Gulf Business*, 5 May 2014; available online at http://gulfbusiness.com/2014/05/facebook-popular-youtube/#.U3o_bPRzamS.

20 Sabbagh et al., "Understanding the Arab Digital Generation," 10.

21 Go-Gulf, "Internet Usage in the Middle East."

22 Mark Lynch, *The Arab Uprisings* (New York: PublicAffairs, 2013), 20.

23 Bruce Etling et al., "Mapping the Arabic Blogosphere: Politics, Culture, and Dissent," Berkman Center Research Publication 2009–06 (Cambridge, MA: Harvard University, Berkman Center for Internet & Society, Internet & Democracy Project, 2009).

24 See Marc Lynch, "Blogging the New Arab Republic," *Arab Media & Society*, February 2007; available online at http://www.arabmediasociety.com/topics/index.php?t_article=32.

25 Ibid.

26 Robert Faris et al., "Online Security in the Middle East and North Africa: A Survey of Perceptions, Knowledge, and Practice" (Cambridge, MA: Harvard University, Berkman Center for Internet & Society Report, August 2011); available online at http://cyber.law.harvard.edu/sites/cyber.law.harvard.edu/files/OnlineSecurityintheMiddleEastandNorthAfrica_August2011.pdf.

27 Etling et al., "Mapping the Arabic Blogosphere."

28 Dubai School of Government, "The Arab World Online: Trends in Internet Usage in the Arab Region," Arab Social Media Report Series, Governance and Innovation Program (Dubai, UAE: Government of Dubai, 2012), 8; available online at http://www.arabsocialmediareport.com/News/description.aspx?NewsID=11.

29 Rory Jones and Ahmed Al Omran, "Saudi Arabia plans to regulate local YouTube content," *Wall Street Journal (Online)*, 24 April 2014; available online at http://www.wsj.com/articles/SB10001424052702304518704579521463293165726.

30 Shediac, Bohsali, and Samman, "Bedrock of Society," 3.

31 Ibid., 26. Yet, the majority of Arabs felt safe in their own country and that they had input into designing its future.

32 Ibid., 34.

33 Bob Rijkers, Caroline Freund, and Antonio Nucifora, "All in the Family: State Capture in Tunisia," World Bank Policy Research Working Paper 6810 (Washington, DC: World Bank Group, 2014).

34 See Madeleine Albright and Steven Cook, "In Support of Arab Democracy: Why and How," Council on Foreign Relations Independent Task Force Report 54 (New York: Council on Foreign Relations, 2005).

35 See Larbu Sadiki, *Rethinking Arab Democratization: Elections without Democracy* (New York: Oxford University Press, 2009).
36 ASDA'A Burson-Marsteller, "Arab Youth Survey 2010/11" (Dubai, UAE: ASDA'A Burson-Marsteller, 2011).
37 Ibid., 21.
38 Kristin Diwan, "Breaking Taboos: Youth Activism in the Gulf States," Atlantic Council Issue Brief (Washington, DC: Atlantic Council of the United States, 2014).
39 Stephen R. Grand, *Understanding Tahrir Square: What Transitions Elsewhere Can Teach Us about the Prospects for Arab Democracy* (Washington, DC: Brookings Institution Press, 2014).

4 Identity

1   For surveys on support of the *hijab* in Arab countries, see "Dress Style Preference and a Woman's Right to Dress as She Wishes" (Ann Arbor: University of Michigan, Population Studies Center, 2013); available online at http://mevs.org/files/tmp/Women_Dress_Demographics.pdf.
2   Population Council, "Survey of Young People in Egypt: Final Report, January 2011" (Cairo: Population Council West Asia and North Africa, 2011), 133; available online at http://www.popcouncil.org/uploads/pdfs/2010PGY_SYPEFinalReport.pdf.
3   Ibid.
4   Marwan Kraidy and Joe Khalil, *Youth, Media and Culture in the Arab World: International Handbook of Children, Media and Culture* (Thousand Oaks, CA: Sage, 2008), 338.
5   Etling et al., "Mapping the Arabic Blogosphere."
6   See Will Kymlicka and Eva Pfastl, eds., *Multiculturalism and Minority Rights in the Arab World* (Oxford: Oxford University Press, 2014).
7   See Shadi Hamid, *Temptations of Power: Islamists and Illiberal Democracy in a New Middle East* (Oxford: Oxford University Press, 2014).
8   Monita Vohra, Gagan Bhalla, and Aurobindo Chowdhury, "Understanding the Islamic Consumer," *Research World* (February 2000): 41.
9   Ibid. I deleted another category, "pragmatic strivers," because it was less applicable to Arab consumers and more to non-Arab Muslim countries such as Indonesia and Malaysia.
10 Mark Tessler, "Islam and the Struggle for a Political Formula: Findings from the 2010–2011 Arab Barometer"; available online at http://www.arabbarometer.org/reports-presentation-abwave/arab-barometer-ii.

11 Pew Research Center, "Pew Research Religion & Public Life Project"
    (Washington, DC, 30 April 2014); available online at http://www
    .pewforum.org/2013/04/30/the-worlds-muslims-religion-politics-
    society-beliefs-about-sharia/.

12 Al Jazeera Center for Studies, "The Arab Spring: Results of the Arab
    Youth Opinion Poll" (Qatar, 30 July 2013); available online at http://
    studies.aljazeera.net/en/reports/2013/07/20137296337455953.htm.

13 Pew Research Center, "The World's Muslims: Religion, Politics and
    Society" (Washington, DC, 30 April 2013); available online at http://
    www.pewforum.org/2013/04/30/the-worlds-muslims-religion-politics-
    society-overview/#extremism-widely-rejected.

14 Mark Tessler, "Popular Views about Islam and Politics in the Arab
    World," *II Journal* (Fall 2011): 1. The results are based on Tessler's
    randomized interviews with 13,019 Arabs in eight countries from 2006
    to 2009.

15 Amaney Jamal and Mark Tessler, "Democracy Barometers: Attitudes in
    the Arab World," *Journal of Democracy* 19, no. 1 (2008): 105.

16 Shediac, Bohsali, and Samman, "Bedrock of Society," 27.

17 James Zogby, "Attitudes of Arabs 2005" (n.p., Zogby International,
    December 2005); available online at http://b.3cdn.net/
    aai/8e7f27fe5092d5bf15_znm6bxbj6.pdf, 9, 10.

18 Richard Shediac et al., "Generations A: Differences and Similarities
    across the Arab Generations" (New York: Booz & Company, 2013), 50;
    available online at http://www.strategyand.pwc.com/global/home/
    what-we-think/reports-white-papers/article-display/arab-generations.
    The results are based on a survey of three thousand Arabs in six coun-
    tries: Egypt, Jordan, Kuwait, Qatar, Saudi Arabia, and the UAE. Women
    had the option of selecting among thirteen responses; percentages do not
    add to a hundred.

19 "Untraditional Choice," *Economist*, 13 July 2013; available online at
    http://www.economist.com/news/business/21581740-middle-east-
    beats-west-female-tech-founders-untraditional-choice.

20 DeAnne Aguirre et al., *Empowering the Third Billion: Women and the World
    of Work in 2012* (New York: Booz & Company, 2012), 66–7; available
    online at http://www.strategyand.pwc.com/global/home/what-we-
    think/reports-white-papers/article-display/empowering-third-billion-
    women-world.

21 Karim Sabbagh, Hatem Samman, and Ramez Shehadi, *Understanding the
    Arab Digital Generation* (New York: Booz & Company, 2012), 2. The nine

countries are Saudi Arabia, the UAE, Egypt, Bahrain, Kuwait, Qatar, Jordan, Algeria, and Lebanon.

22 Julie De Jong and Mansoor Moaddel, "Trends in Values among Saudi Youth: Findings from Values Surveys," *Journal of the History of Childhood and Youth* 6, no. 1 (2013): 151–64.

23 See Diana Baumrind, "Effects of Authoritative Parental Control on Child Behavior," *Child Development* 37, no. 4 (1966): 887–907, who used these classifications to describe changing parenting styles.

24 Ruth Hill Useem and Richard D. Downie, "Third-Culture Kids," *Today's Education* 65, no. 3 (1976): 103–5.

25 ASDA'A Burson-Marsteller, "Arab Youth Survey 2010/11"; the nine countries surveyed were the UAE, Oman, Qatar, Bahrain, Saudi Arabia, Kuwait, Egypt, Jordan, and Lebanon.

26 Pew Research Center, "World's Muslims."

27 "The man behind Khawater offers words of wisdom," *Saudi Gazette*, 10 August, 2010; available online at http://www.saudigazette.com.sa/index.cfm?method=home.regcon&contentID=2010081080620; emphasis added.

28 See Robert Worth, "Preaching moderate Islam and becoming a TV star," *New York Times*, 2 January 2009; available online at http://www.nytimes.com/2009/01/03/world/middleeast/03preacher.html?pagewanted=1&_r=0&partner=rss&emc=rss#.

5 Circularity

1 Louise Cainkar, "Global Arab World Migrations and Diasporas," *Arab Studies Journal* 21, no. 1 (2013): 133–5.

2 Ibid., 133.

3 Ibid., 151.

4 Ibid., 140.

5 See Tim Cresswell, "Towards a Politics of Mobility," *Environment and Planning D: Society and Space* 28, no. 1 (2010): 18.

6 Louise Cainkar, "The Social Construction of Difference and the Arab American Experience," *Journal of American Ethnic History* 25, nos. 2–3 (2006): 243–78.

7 See Cainkar, "Global Arab World Migrations and Diasporas," 133. The original sources are Angela Brittingham and G. Patricia de la Cruz, *We the People of Arab Ancestry in the United States* (Washington, DC: Department of Commerce, Census Bureau, 2005); and Colin Lindsay,

"The Arab Community in Canada 2001," cat. no. 89-621-XIE – no. 9 (Ottawa: Statistics Canada, 2007), available online at http://www .statcan.gc.ca/pub/89-621-x/89-621-x2007009-eng.pdf.

8 Steven Vertovec, "Conceiving and Researching Transnationalism," *Ethnic and Racial Studies* 22, no. 2 (1999): 447–62.

9 Manuel Castells, *The Information Age: Economy, Society, and Culture*, vol. 2, *The Power of Identity*, 2nd ed. (New York: Wiley, 2003).

10 A total of ninety-two respondents completed the survey, nearly evenly split between males and females. The average respondent was twenty-four years old. Analysis was done using descriptive statistics, means testing, analysis of variance, and linear regressions methods. For the analysis, statistical significance occurred outside a 90 per cent confidence interval, and substantive significance occurred when the effect of a statistical relationship was large enough to affect the variable in question; the adjusted R-squared values of the models were also considered where applicable.

11 International Institute of Education, "Open Doors Data: International Students, All Places of Origin" (n.p., 2014), available online at http:// www.iie.org/Research-and-Publications/Open-Doors/Data/International-Students/All-Places-of-Origin; and Caroline R. Nagel and Lynn A. Staeheli, "Citizenship, Identity and Transnational Migration: Arab Immigrants to the United States," *Space and Polity* 8, no. 1 (2004): 3–23.

12 B. Zahlan, "Higher Education, R&D, Economic Development, Regional and Global Interface" (paper presented at the Regional Seminar, "The Impact of Globalization on Higher Education and Research in the Arab States," Rabat, Morocco, 24–25 May 2007).

13 UNESCO, Institute for Statistics, "International Student Mobility in Tertiary Education" (Paris, 2014); available online at http://data.uis .unesco.org/Index.aspx?queryid=170, accessed 20 October 2014.

14 Peggy Levitt and Deepak Lamba-Nieves, "Social Remittances Revisited," *Journal of Ethnic and Migration Studies* 37, no. 1 (2011): 1–22.

15 Laura Bashraheel, "Scholarship students: Big dreams, slow change," *Saudi Gazette*, 11 March 2013; available online at http://www.saudigazette .com.sa/index.cfm?method=home.regcon&contentid=20130311156300.

16 Ibid.

17 Mohammed bin Rashid Al Maktoum Foundation and UNDP, *Arab Knowledge Report: Towards Productive Intercommunication for Knowledge* (Dubai, UAE, 2009); available online at http://www.undp.org/content/ dam/rbas/report/ahdr/AKR2009-Eng-Full-Report.pdf.

18 AnnaLee Saxenian, "From Brain Drain to Brain Circulation: Transnational Communities and Regional Upgrading in India and China," *Studies in Comparative International Development* 40, no. 2 (2005): 35–61.

19 Heba Nassar, "Recent Trends of Egyptian Migration," CARIM Analytic and Synthetic Notes 2011/72 (San Domenico di Fiesole, Italy: European University Institute, Robert Schuman Centre for Advanced Studies, 2011).

20 See Population Council, "Migration Aspirations and Experiences of Egyptian Youth" (Cairo: Population Council West Asia and North Africa, February 2011); and Barry McCormick and Jackline Wahba, "Return International Migration and Geographical Inequality: The Case of Egypt," *Journal of African Economies* 12, no. 4 (2003): 500–32.

21 See Jackline Wahba and Yves Zenou, "Out of Sight, Out of Mind: Migration, Entrepreneurship and Social Capital," *Regional Science and Urban Economics* 42, no. 5 (2012): 890–903; Jackline Wahba, "Returns to Overseas Work Experience: The Case of Egypt," in *International Migration, Economic Development, and Policy*, ed. Maurice Schiff and Caglar Ozden, 235–58 (Washington, DC: World Bank, 2007); and Nadine Sika, "Highly-Skilled Migration Patterns and Development: The Case of Egypt," CARIM Analytic and Synthetic Notes 2010/17 (San Domenico di Fiesole, Italy: European University Institute, Robert Schuman Centre for Advanced Studies, 2010).

22 International Organization for Migration, "Migration Aspirations and Experiences of Egyptian Youth" (Cairo, 2011), 6.

23 Ibid., 6–7.

24 Flore Gubert and Christophe J. Nordman, "Return Migration and Small Enterprise Development in the Maghreb," in *Diaspora for Development in Africa*, ed. Sonia Plaza and Dilip Ratha (Washington, DC: World Bank, 2011), 119.

25 See http://blog.linkedin.com/2014/05/20/careers-that-will-move-you-what-it-takes-to-work-around-the-world/.

26 Anisur Rahman, "Migration and Human Rights in the Gulf," in *Migration and the Gulf* (Washington, DC: Middle East Institute, 2010), 16–19.

27 Wael Ghonim, interview with *Dream TV*, 7 February 2011; available online at https://www.youtube.com/watch?v=yW59LZsjE_g.

6 Conclusion

1 Navtej Dhillon, Paul Dyer, and Tarik Yousef, "Generation in Waiting: An Overview of School to Work and Family Formation Transitions," in

Generation in Waiting: The Unfulfilled Promise of Young People in the Middle East, ed. Navtej Dhillon and Tarik Yousef (Washington, DC: Brookings Institution Press), 34–5.

2 Elena Ianchovichina and Susanna Lundstrom, "Inclusive Growth Analytics: Framework and Application," Policy Research Working Paper Series 4851 (Washington, DC: World Bank, 2009).

3 Dhillon, Dyer, and Yousef, "Generation in Waiting," 34–5.

4 International Monetary Fund (IMF), *Regional Economic Outlook, April 2011: Middle East and Central Asia* (Washington, DC: IMF, 2011), 42.

5 These last two points were inspired by Rami Khouri, "Beyond Sunnis and Shiites" (speech to the Canadian Arab Institute, Toronto, 29 October 2014); available online at http://www.canadianarabinstitute.org/events/pas/perspectives-changing-middle-east/khouri/.

6 IMF, "Economic Transformation in MENA: Delivering on the Promise of Shared Prosperity" (presentation to the G-8 Summit, Deauville, France, 27 May 2011).

7 Ibid.

8 World Bank, *Transforming Arab Economies: Traveling the Knowledge and Innovation Road* (Washington, DC, 2013), 113.

9 Joanna Slater, "The new frontier Mideast," *Wall Street Journal*, 4 April 2007.

10 Gholamreza Mansourfar, Shamsher Mohamad, and Taufiq Hassan, "The Behavior of MENA Oil and Non-Oil Producing Countries in International Portfolio Optimization," *Quarterly Review of Economics and Finance* 50, no. 4 (2010): 415–23.

11 Simeon Kerr, "Equities soar as confidence returns to Arab stock markets," *Financial Times*, 8 October 2014; available online at http://www.ft.com/cms/s/0/437e141c-3fe8-11e4-936b-00144feabdc0.html#ixzz3KN9niio3.

12 Chedly Ayari, "Building the Future: Jobs, Growth, & Fairness in the Arab World" (presentation to the conference, "Building the Future: Jobs, Growth, and Fairness in the Arab World," Amman, Jordan, 11–12 May 2014); available online at http://www.imf.org/external/np/seminars/eng/2014/act/.

13 See IMF, *Toward New Horizons: Arab Economic Transformation mid Political Transitions* (Washington, DC: IMF, Middle East and Central Asia Department, 2014), 47–50.

14 Ibid., 41.

15 Adnan Ahmad Youssef, "Islamic banking on the rise," *Al-Monitor*, 30 October 2014; available online at http://www.al-monitor.com/pulse/business/2014/10/islamic-bank-sector-arab-west.html.

16 See Vali Nasr, "Business, Not as Usual," *Finance and Development* (International Monetary Fund), March 2013, 26–9; available online at http://www.imf.org/external/pubs/ft/fandd/2013/03/pdf/nasr.pdf.

17 Patrick Imam and Kangni Kpodar, "Islamic Banking: How Has It Diffused?" IMF Working Paper WP/10/195 (Washington, DC: International Monetary Fund, 2010), 20; available online at https://www.imf.org/external/pubs/ft/wp/2010/wp10195.pdf.

18 See Yasser Abdin, "Closing the Jobs Gap," *Finance and Development* (International Monetary Fund), June 2011, 38.

19 Ivan Woods and Holly Hyde, "Prospects for PPPs in the Middle East," *International Financing Review* (2011); available online at http://www.ifre.com/prospects-for-ppps-in-the-middle-east/1611517.fullarticle, accessed 26 August 2012.

20 Booz & Company, "Building the Digital Middle East: 2011 ICT Leaders' Event" (n.p., 2011); available online at http://strategyand.pwc.com/media/uploads/Strategyand-Building-Digital-Middle-East-ICT.pdf.

21 United Nations Economic and Social Commission for Western Asia, "Status of the Digital Arabic Content Industry in the Arab Region" (Beirut, 2012); available online at http://www.escwa.un.org/information/publications/edit/upload/E_ESCWA_ICTD_12_TP-4_E.pdf.

22 Jordan, *Jordan National Information And Communications Technology Strategy (2013–2017)* (n.p.: n.d.); available online at http://www.intaj.net/sites/default/files/jordan_nis_june_2013.pdf.

23 Masoud Imani-Kalesar, "Developing Arab-Islamic Tourism in the Middle East: An Economic Benefit or a Cultural Seclusion?" *International Politics* 3, no. 5 (2010): 106–36.

24 Saj Ahmad, "No signs of slowing for Emirates," *Khaleej Times*, 18 November 2014; available online at http://www.khaleejtimes.com/article/20141118/ARTICLE/311189876/1036.

25 See Michael Hoffman, "Attitudes towards Religious Minorities in the Arab World" (Washington, DC: Georgetown University, Berkley Center for Religion, Peace & World Affairs, 27 August 2014); available online at http://berkleycenter.georgetown.edu/cornerstone/global-christian-persecution/responses/attitudes-towards-religious-minorities-in-the-arab-world.

26 See Pew Research Center, "Concerns about Islamic Extremism on the Rise in Middle East" (Washington, DC, July 2014).

27 Palestinian Center for Policy and Survey Research, "Palestinian Public Opinion Poll No (55)," Press release, 24 March 2015; available online at http://pcpsr.org/en/node/603.

28 Arab Center for Research & Policy Studies, "The Military Campaign against the Islamic State in Iraq and the Levant: Arab Public Opinion" (Doha, Qatar: Doha Institute for Graduate Studies, 11 November 2014); available online at http://english.dohainstitute.org/file/Get/40ebdf12-8960-4d18-8088-7c8a077e522e.

29 Juan Cole, *The New Arabs: How the Millennial Generation Is Changing the Middle East* (New York: Simon & Schuster, 2014).

30 Marwan Muasher, *The Second Arab Awakening: And the Battle for Pluralism* (New Haven, CT: Yale University Press, 2014).

Lightning Source UK Ltd.
Milton Keynes UK
UKOW02f1236030616

275536UK00001B/184/P